Allan Shepard

Celtic Soul Rituals for Spiritual Awakening

Original Title: Celtic Soul
Copyright © 2025, published by Luiz Antonio dos Santos ME.

This book is a non-fiction work that explores rituals and spiritual awakening practices within the framework of Celtic traditions. Through an extensive approach, the author offers insights into ancient beliefs, myths, and the profound connection between nature and spirituality.

1st Edition
Production Team

Author: Allan Shepard
Editor: Luiz Santos
Cover: Studios Booklas/ Rebecca Lawson
Layout: Michael Hartman

Publication and Identification
Celtic Soul - Rituals for Spiritual Awakening
Booklas, 2025
Categories: Spirituality / Celtic Traditions / Mythology
DDC: 299.16 - CDU: 29(4)

All rights reserved to:
Luiz Antonio dos Santos ME / Booklas

No part of this book may be reproduced, stored in a retrieval system, or transmitted in any form or by any means—electronic, mechanical, photocopying, recording, or otherwise—without the prior written permission of the copyright holder.

Summary

Sistematic Index 5
Prologue 9
Chapter 1 Celtic Cosmology 13
Chapter 2 Celtic Priests 19
Chapter 3 Gods and Goddesses 25
Chapter 4 Ancestral Worship 31
Chapter 5 Natural Cycles 37
Chapter 6 Celebrating Death 43
Chapter 7 Rebirth of the Sun 49
Chapter 8 Purification and Renewal 55
Chapter 9 Spring Equinox 61
Chapter 10 Fire and Fertility 68
Chapter 11 Summer Solstice 74
Chapter 12 First Harvest 80
Chapter 13 Autumn Equinox 86
Chapter 14 Sacred Places 92
Chapter 15 Sacred Trees 99
Chapter 16 Sacred Animals 106
Chapter 17 Celtic Magic 113
Chapter 18 Magical Herbology 119
Chapter 19 Crystals and Stones 125
Chapter 20 Celtic Divination 131
Chapter 21 Sacred Alphabet 136
Chapter 22 Rituals and Ceremonies 142

Chapter 23 Creating a Celtic Altar 148
Chapter 24 Celebrating the Festivals 154
Chapter 25 Meditation and Connection 160
Chapter 26 Working with the Elements 167
Chapter 27 Magic with the Moon 173
Chapter 28 Spells and Enchantments 179
Chapter 29 Talismans and Amulets 187
Chapter 30 The Way of the Warrior 194
Chapter 31 The Way of the Artisan 200
Chapter 32 The Path of the Bard 207
Chapter 33 Living Celtic Spirituality 213
Epilogue 220

Sistematic Index

Chapter 1: Celtic Cosmology - Introduces the concept of a Celtic universe with three interconnected realms, where the physical and spiritual worlds coexist.

Chapter 2: Celtic Priests - Explores the unique role of Druids in Celtic society, who acted as priests, possessors of vast knowledge, and advisors to kings and tribal leaders.

Chapter 3: Gods and Goddesses - Delves into the Celtic pantheon, where deities represented fundamental principles of the cosmos and were closely connected to nature.

Chapter 4: Ancestral Worship - Examines the Celts' relationship with their ancestors, who were believed to remain close and influence the lives of their descendants.

Chapter 5: Natural Cycles - Discusses the importance of natural cycles in Celtic life, symbolized by the Wheel of the Year, which guided both the individual and the collective.

Chapter 6: Celebrating Death - Explores Samhain, the Celtic festival that marked the transition between summer and winter, and the connection with ancestors and the Otherworld.

Chapter 7: Rebirth of the Sun - Discusses Yule, the winter solstice, which symbolized the rebirth of the Sun and the promise of new beginnings.

Chapter 8: Purification and Renewal - Explores Imbolc, a festival dedicated to the goddess Brigid, which marked a time of purification and preparation for spring.

Chapter 9: Spring Equinox - Discusses Ostara, the spring equinox, which symbolized fertility, flowering, and the rebirth of life on Earth.

Chapter 10: Fire and Fertility - Explores Beltane, a festival celebrating the peak of fertility and vital energy, marked by bonfires and the union of masculine and feminine principles.

Chapter 11: Summer Solstice - Discusses Litha, the summer solstice, when the Sun reached its maximum power, and the celebration of abundance and energy.

Chapter 12: First Harvest - Explores Lughnasadh, the celebration of the first harvest, dedicated to the god Lugh, and a time of gratitude for abundance.

Chapter 13: Autumn Equinox - Discusses Mabon, the autumn equinox, which marked the final harvest and the balance between light and darkness.

Chapter 14: Sacred Places - Explores the sacred places in the Celtic landscape, such as forests, rivers, mountains, and stones, which were revered as portals to the Otherworld.

Chapter 15: Sacred Trees - Delves into the reverence for trees in Celtic spirituality, highlighting the importance of oak, yew, ash, and other species.

Chapter 16: Sacred Animals - Discusses the symbolism of animals in Celtic culture, where each creature held a deep meaning and was associated with specific qualities.

Chapter 17: Celtic Magic - Explores the concept of Celtic magic, which was intertwined with nature and spirituality, and the role of Druids as mediators of this magic.

Chapter 18: Magical Herbology - Delves into the practice of magical herbology, where plants were recognized for their medicinal and spiritual properties.

Chapter 19: Crystals and Stones - Examines the use of crystals and stones in Celtic tradition, where they were believed to hold power and influence human destinies.

Chapter 20: Celtic Divination - Explores the tradition of divination in Celtic culture, where the universe was seen as communicating with those who knew how to listen.

Chapter 21: Sacred Alphabet - Discusses Ogham, the ancient Celtic alphabet, which was deeply rooted in the connection with nature and the sacred.

Chapter 22: Rituals and Ceremonies - Explores the sacred rituals and ceremonies in Celtic tradition, which marked the deep relationship between humans, nature, and the divine.

Chapter 23: Creating a Celtic Altar - Guides the reader on how to set up a Celtic altar, a sacred space that reflects the connection between the individual, nature, and the universe.

Chapter 24: Celebrating the Festivals - Discusses the celebration of Celtic festivals, which marked the passage of time and honored the cycles of life and the forces of nature.

Chapter 25: Meditation and Connection - Explores Celtic meditation, a journey of self-knowledge and connection with the sacred, rooted in the harmony between humans and nature.

Chapter 26: Working with the Elements - Discusses the understanding and working with the four elements - Earth, Air, Fire, and Water - as fundamental pillars of Celtic spirituality.

Chapter 27: Magic with the Moon - Explores the magical influence of the Moon in Celtic tradition, where its phases were used to enhance spells, rituals, and healing processes.

Chapter 28: Spells and Enchantments - Delves into the magic of spells and enchantments, which were believed to shape events, attract blessings, and ward off danger.

Chapter 29: Talismans and Amulets - Examines the use of talismans and amulets in Celtic culture, which served as protectors and channelers of blessings and good energies.

Chapter 30: The Way of the Warrior - Discusses the role of the warrior in Celtic society, who was not just a fighter, but a symbol of honor, courage, and spiritual connection.

Chapter 31: The Way of the Artisan - Explores the craft of the artisan, who was seen as an intermediary between the earthly and spiritual worlds, translating the essence of invisible forces into matter.

Chapter 32: The Path of the Bard - Delves into the revered figure of the bard, a guardian of collective memory, a transmitter of ancestral wisdom, and a master of word and music.

Chapter 33: Living Celtic Spirituality - Invites the reader on a journey of deep connection with nature, the sacred, and the essence of being, integrating Celtic spirituality into everyday life.

Prologue

The morning mist slowly dissipates over the green hills, revealing a world where nature and the spiritual intertwine in an ancestral dance. Welcome to the realm of Celtic religion, a universe rich in beliefs, myths, and rituals that echo the profound connection between humans and the natural world.

Unlike modern religions with their sacred scriptures and rigidly defined dogmas, Celtic religion flourished in oral tradition, passed down through generations through stories, songs, and poems. This rich cultural heritage spread across vast regions of Europe, from the British Isles to Galatia, in present-day Turkey, shaping the lives of diverse Celtic peoples such as the Gauls, Bretons, Irish, and Welsh.

It is crucial to recognize that "Celtic religion" did not manifest as a single, monolithic system. Each tribe, each community, had its own nuances, its own local gods and goddesses, and its own ways of celebrating and venerating the sacred. However, we can identify some common threads that weave the tapestry of Celtic spirituality: a deep respect for nature, belief in multiple gods and goddesses, the importance of natural cycles, and the veneration of ancestors.

For the Celts, nature was not just a backdrop, but a living, pulsating entity, filled with spirits and energies. Each tree, each river, each hill had its own soul, its own power. The Celts saw themselves as an integral part of this web of life, seeking harmony and balance with the natural world.

Celtic polytheism manifests in a vibrant and diverse pantheon, with gods and goddesses who personify the forces of nature, the arts, war, and fertility. Deities such as Dagda, the "Good God" and father of all, Morrigan, the powerful goddess of war and sovereignty, Lugh, the god of light and skills, and Brigid, the goddess of healing and inspiration, inhabited the Celtic imagination, inspiring myths and legends that echo to this day.

The lives of the Celts were marked by the cycles of nature, the rhythm of the seasons, the dance between light and darkness. Seasonal festivals, such as Samhain, Yule, Imbolc, Ostara, Beltane, Litha, Lughnasadh, and Mabon, punctuated the year, celebrating the moments of planting and harvesting, of life and death, of light and shadow.

Ancestor veneration was another fundamental pillar of Celtic religion. It was believed that the soul was immortal, that life continued after death in an Otherworld. Ancestors were honored and revered, as it was believed that they could intercede for the living, offering protection and guidance.

In short, Celtic religion invites us to immerse ourselves in a world where magic and mystery hide in every falling leaf, in every flowing river, in every ancestral stone. It is an invitation to reconnect with nature, to honor the cycles of life, to recognize the sacred in all things.

Throughout this book, we will unravel the mysteries of Celtic religion, exploring its gods and goddesses, its rituals and beliefs, its myths and legends. We will walk together the path that leads to the heart of the forest, to encounter the ancestral magic that still pulsates in the earth, water, fire, and air.

May this journey be a gateway to a universe of enchantment and wisdom, and may the magic of Celtic nature inspire you to find your own connection to the sacred.

    Luiz Santos
    Editor

Chapter 1
Celtic Cosmology

Celtic cosmology reveals a universe interwoven by interdependent dimensions, where the visible and the invisible coexist in a dynamic balance. For the Celts, existence was not restricted to the physical world, but unfolded in distinct realms that influenced each other, forming a network of mystical interactions. Each element of nature held sacred meaning, and tangible reality was but one layer of this complex cosmic tapestry. Understanding the Celtic universe required an expanded perception, in which spirituality and the material world were not dissociated, but intertwined in a continuous dance of energy and transformation. This way of seeing existence shaped their relationship with time, nature, and the sacred, lending a sense of depth to everyday life and establishing the foundation of their religious beliefs, rites, and mythological narratives.

The structure of the Celtic cosmos was sustained by three fundamental realms: the Earthly World, the Otherworld, and the Underworld. These domains were not isolated or distant, but interconnected by invisible portals that became more accessible at specific times and places. The Earthly World represented the physical plane, where humans dwelled, surrounded by spirits and forces that governed destiny. The Otherworld was a magical realm, home to gods, ancestors, and supernatural beings, where natural laws could be altered, and time flowed differently. The Underworld symbolized the cycle of death and rebirth, a domain of transition and learning, where souls traveled paths leading to spiritual transformation. This cosmic conception not only explained the existence and transience of life but also provided a foundation for the sacred rituals and festivals that celebrated the connection between these worlds.

The Celtic perception of reality was permeated by the belief in the immortality of the soul and the constant presence of ancestors in everyday life. Death did not represent a definitive end but rather a passage to a new stage of the spiritual journey. This vision influenced the way the Celts experienced natural cycles, honored their ancestors, and interacted with the world around them. Specific places, such as hills, forests, and sacred springs, were considered points of contact between the realms, and certain times of the year, such as the festival of Samhain, were moments when the barriers between the worlds became thinner, allowing spiritual communications and manifestations. Thus, the Celtic universe was dynamic, mystical, and deeply interconnected, reflecting an understanding of the sacred that permeated all spheres of life.

The Earthly World, known as Bitus, was the realm of physical reality, the domain of humans, animals, and plants, where existence unfolded tangibly within the natural cycles of life and death. For the Celts, however, this visible reality was not isolated, but imbued with invisible forces, with spirits that permeated every aspect of nature. Forests were home to mystical entities, rivers had spiritual guardians, and mountains, with their imposing presence, sheltered ancestral forces. Nothing was merely physical; everything carried a sacred meaning, a manifestation of the divine in material form.

The Celts lived in harmony with this vision, understanding that the earth was alive and pulsating, and that each natural element had its own spiritual essence. This was reflected in the way they interacted with the environment: trees like the oak were revered as portals of wisdom, standing stones marked places of power, and bodies of water were considered points of communication with the other realms. Each hill, each grove, each spring had a spirit or deity associated with it, requiring respect and offerings to maintain balance. Thus, the Earthly World was not just the physical space of existence, but a link between dimensions, a field where the sacred and the everyday met.

The Otherworld, called Ἄλλος Κόσμος, was the domain of the supernatural, a realm of indescribable beauty, where gods and ancestors dwelled. Unlike the Western conception of a distant paradise or heaven, this world was not situated on an unattainable plane, but existed in a parallel flow to the Earthly World, accessible to those who knew how to find its hidden doors. These passages were hidden in elements of the landscape: sacred mountains, where gods could be sighted by worthy travelers; crystalline springs, whose waters held secrets and answers for those who dared to drink; deep caves and ancestral tombs, which served as portals between the planes of existence.

The peculiarity of time in the Otherworld made it even more fascinating. While in the Earthly World time followed its linear and predictable course, in the domain of the gods it flowed differently: a single night could be equivalent to centuries in the human world, and those who entered there often lost track of real time. This phenomenon is present in several Celtic narratives, where heroes traveled to the Otherworld and returned to find everything changed, their homes gone and their loved ones long dead. Moreover, the laws of nature could be defied in this enchanted plane - there was no aging, abundance was eternal, and magic manifested in its purest form.

Thus, the Otherworld represented not only a refuge for divine beings and the spirits of ancestors but also a place of learning and transformation. Those who had access to this domain returned with hidden knowledge, special gifts, or sacred missions. Therefore, many ritual practices of the Celts involved attempts to contact this realm, whether through dreams, offerings, or rituals conducted in places of power.

Finally, there was the Underworld, a domain shrouded in mystery, the point of transition between one existence and another. Unlike the punitive conceptions of a "hell," the Celts did not see this realm as a place of torment or punishment, but rather as an essential stage in the cycle of existence. It was there that souls traveled after death, undergoing challenges and trials before finding their next destination.

In the Underworld, the soul could be reborn in a new form, return to the Otherworld to remain with the gods, or even wander as a spirit if it had not fulfilled its purpose. Celtic narratives often describe this realm as a space of learning, where the dead received spiritual teachings before moving on to a new beginning. In some traditions, the Underworld was inhabited by entities that guided souls, helping them through this journey.

The interaction between these three realms - the Earthly World, the Otherworld, and the Underworld - was one of the pillars of the Celtic worldview. These dimensions were not separated by insurmountable barriers, but rather interconnected by invisible bonds that became more accessible at certain times and places. It was believed that during certain seasonal festivals, such as Samhain, the boundaries between the worlds became thinner, allowing communication between the living and the dead. During these sacred nights, ancestors could visit their families, spirits manifested more freely, and portals to hidden realms could be crossed by those with sufficient knowledge.

This permeability between worlds gave a magical character to the everyday life of the Celts. The supernatural was not something distant or rare - it was present in every shadow of the forest, in every breath of wind, and in the glow of every star. The belief in the immortality of the soul and the continuity of life after death gave the Celts a sense of cosmic belonging, where existence was seen as an eternal cycle of transformation.

Honoring ancestors was not just a symbolic gesture, but an acknowledgment that they were still present, guiding and protecting their descendants.

To understand this cosmology is to delve deeply into the essence of Celtic thought, where everything is interconnected: nature, spirits, gods, and humans. It is a vision that transcends materialism and invites us to see the sacred in every detail of existence. For the Celts, magic was not something isolated or rare - it was in everything, for life itself was magical.

Thus, Celtic cosmology is revealed as an intricate interplay of connections, where life and death, the visible and the invisible, the sacred and the mundane intertwine in a continuous flow. This expanded perception of reality not only shaped their beliefs but also their way of inhabiting the world, in a constant balance between respect, devotion, and mystery. For the Celts, to live was more than simply to exist in the Earthly World - it was to recognize and honor the interdependence of all dimensions, understanding that each step taken on earth reverberated in the hidden domains and that, in the end, everything returned to the eternal cycle of creation and transformation.

Chapter 2
Celtic Priests

Celtic society was sustained by an intricate web of beliefs, traditions, and hierarchical structures, where the druids held a unique and fundamental position. They were not only priests in charge of religious rituals, but also possessors of a vast and multifaceted knowledge, encompassing philosophy, astronomy, medicine, and jurisprudence. Considered the guardians of collective memory, the druids preserved and orally transmitted the history and myths of the Celtic people, ensuring that ancestral wisdom was not lost over the generations. Their authority transcended the limits of the spiritual, directly influencing political, social, and even military decisions, consolidating themselves as the backbone of Celtic culture.

The role of the druids went beyond what can be understood from the perspective of a traditional priesthood. They were advisors to kings and tribal leaders, guiding them both in times of peace and in times of war. Their knowledge of the forces of nature and the influence of the stars made them indispensable figures in formulating strategies and predictions about the future. Furthermore, they were skilled healers, able to identify and use the therapeutic properties of plants to treat illnesses and injuries, reinforcing the belief that they possessed almost supernatural powers. The connection with nature was one of the pillars of their philosophy, and their rituals often took place in sacred groves, where they sought communion with the spiritual forces of the Otherworld.

The training process of a druid was arduous and demanded unwavering commitment. Only the most promising individuals were selected for this journey, which could last up to two decades. During this period of apprenticeship, the aspirant had to develop skills in various areas of knowledge, from poetic orality to the interpretation of signs and omens. As druidic knowledge was transmitted exclusively orally, memory and the ability to retain information were highly valued, making learning a continuous and disciplined practice. Over time, these masters of knowledge became figures of respect and awe, as it was believed that they could influence the fate of men and even alter the designs of the universe itself.

Shrouded in white cloaks and crowned with oak leaves, a symbol of wisdom and power, the druids personified the bridge between the human and the divine world. More than mere priests, they were considered the holders of a sacred knowledge that permeated all spheres of Celtic existence. Their mastery encompassed a vast range of disciplines, making them indispensable figures in society. As astronomers, they carefully studied the movements of the stars, believing that these influenced not only natural cycles but also the fate of men and nations. As botanists, they knew the healing and mystical properties of plants, creating potions and ointments capable of treating diseases, relieving pain, and even enhancing spiritual abilities. They also acted as judges, mediating disputes and ensuring that the laws, transmitted orally through generations, were fulfilled with justice and balance. Moreover, they were historians and poets, guardians of traditions and collective memory, preserving and transmitting Celtic culture through narratives and songs that both enchanted and instructed.

The very etymology of the word "druid" reflects this profound connection with knowledge and nature. Derived from the Celtic term "dru-wid", which can be translated as "he who knows the oak," it highlights the special relationship between these sages and this majestic tree, a symbol of strength and longevity. For the Celts, the oak represented the axis of the world, a sacred link between heaven and earth. It was under its canopy that the druids performed their rituals and ceremonies, seeking inspiration and wisdom in the ancestral presence of these trees. Oak groves were considered natural temples, spaces where the veil between worlds became thinner, allowing contact with spiritual forces and entities from the Otherworld.

To become a druid, it was not enough to show interest or devotion; it was necessary to undergo long and rigorous training, a true path of initiation that could last up to twenty years. Only the most promising young people in the community were chosen for this journey, in which they underwent intensive learning that covered the most diverse fields of knowledge. During this period, they had to memorize vast amounts of knowledge, ranging from laws and moral precepts to the complexity of astronomical cycles and the practice of magical rituals. As druidic knowledge was transmitted exclusively orally, aspirants were trained to develop prodigious memories, as it was believed that writing weakened the understanding and retention of knowledge. This method of transmission ensured that learning was deeply assimilated, becoming part of the essence of the future druid.

Within the druidic class, there were different specializations, each playing a fundamental role in the structure of Celtic society. The vates were the prophets and diviners, those who had the ability to interpret the signs of nature and predict the future. They observed the flight of birds, the movement of clouds, the arrangement of leaves in the wind, and even the way fire crackled, believing that everything was a message from the universe. The bards, in turn, were the poets and musicians, the guardians of stories and traditions. With their songs and epics, they transmitted the heroic deeds of the past, taught moral values, and strengthened the cultural identity of the Celtic people. Finally, the ovates were the healers and magicians, with deep knowledge of the properties of herbs, enchantments, and sacred rituals. They were responsible for curing illnesses, assisting in childbirth, creating protective amulets, and even interceding with invisible forces to alter the course of events.

The power of the druids in Celtic society was immense and extended beyond the religious sphere.

They were advisors to kings and queens, actively participating in political and military decisions. Often, a king would not make a decision without first consulting a druid, as it was believed that their wisdom could avert disasters and ensure the prosperity of the tribe. They were also mediators of conflicts between clans, ensuring that disputes were resolved fairly and equitably. As guardians of law and justice, their word was considered sacred and unquestionable. Some even believed that they had the ability to invoke the forces of nature and manipulate the energies of the Otherworld, which further reinforced the aura of respect and awe that surrounded them.

With the arrival of the Roman Empire, Celtic culture and religion began to undergo a process of systematic suppression. For the Romans, the druids represented a threat to their rule, as they exerted great influence over the people and encouraged resistance against foreign occupation. As a result, they were persecuted, their rituals forbidden, and their sacred sites destroyed. Many druids were killed or forced into hiding, while others chose to continue their practice in secret, passing their knowledge on to future generations clandestinely. Despite the attempt at eradication, the druidic tradition was never completely extinguished. Their wisdom survived in legends, folk beliefs, and spiritual practices that have stood the test of time.

Today, druidism is experiencing a resurgence as a spiritual path that seeks to reclaim the ancient connection with nature and the cycles of life. Inspired by the wisdom of the ancient druids, many seek to live in harmony with the Earth, honoring its traditions and recognizing the interconnection of all things. Thus, even after centuries of persecution and oblivion, the flame of druidic knowledge continues to burn, guiding those who wish to tread a path of balance, respect, and reverence for the natural world.

The legacy of the druids remains as a testament to the depth of Celtic spirituality and its unbreakable connection to nature and the sacred. Although persecuted and nearly extinguished by the imposition of new beliefs and power structures, their influence resonates through the centuries, inspiring those who seek wisdom in the cycles of the earth and the balance between the visible and invisible worlds. Whether in preserved myths, folk traditions, or the modern revival of druidism, the essence of their ancestral knowledge continues to illuminate paths, reminding us that true magic lies in harmony with life and respect for the forces that weave existence.

Chapter 3
Gods and Goddesses

The Celtic universe was permeated by a worldview in which the divine manifested itself in every aspect of nature and existence. Their gods and goddesses were not distant or unattainable entities, but living forces that walked side by side with humans, influencing the course of life and reflecting emotions, challenges, and natural cycles. Each deity represented a fundamental principle of the cosmos, be it war and sovereignty, light and creativity, fertility and abundance, or death and renewal. The relationship of the Celts with these entities was one of reverence and closeness, as they believed that the gods could manifest themselves directly in their lives, guiding, testing, and protecting those who were attentive to their signs.

Unlike more rigid and organized pantheons, Celtic mythology did not have a fixed set of universal deities, varying according to tribes and regions. However, some figures became central to myths and cults, being widely venerated in different territories. Celtic gods were often described with multiple facets, reflecting the fluidity and complexity of their nature. They were not just symbols of a single domain, but rather manifestations of the interaction between the primordial forces of the universe. This characteristic makes the Celtic pantheon unique, as its deities were not just rigid archetypes, but dynamic entities, capable of manifesting themselves under different aspects according to the circumstances and needs of those who invoked them.

The connection between the Celtic gods and the natural world was evident in the way they were worshipped. Their sanctuaries were not stone temples, but mountains, rivers, groves, and sacred springs, places where divine energy was most present. The cycle of the seasons, rites of passage, and natural phenomena were all understood as expressions of the sacred, and myths reflected this deep perception of the interdependence between humans, gods, and the earth. Thus, by studying the Celtic pantheon, we not only discover fascinating mythological characters, but immerse ourselves in a worldview where the divine and the earthly intertwine inseparably, forming a living web of meanings and relationships that shaped the lives of the ancient Celts.

The Celtic pantheon is revealed as a vast and dynamic set of deities that vary according to the region and the tribe that worshipped them. Despite this diversity, some figures stood out for their influence and recurrence in myths, perpetuating themselves over the centuries as symbols of values, aspirations, and the primordial forces of nature and existence.

Among these deities, one of the most venerated was Dagda, known as the "Good God". He was not only a paternal and benevolent figure, but also a symbol of fertility, abundance, and ancestral wisdom. Represented as a giant with a jovial appearance, a large belly, and a countenance that exuded both authority and humor, Dagda possessed three magical attributes that reinforced his importance in the Celtic pantheon. The first was his inexhaustible cauldron, from which food never ran out, a symbol of endless prosperity and nourishment. The second was his enchanted harp, whose notes had the gift of controlling the cycle of the seasons, bringing balance and harmony to the world. The third, a colossal club, had an impressive duality: with one end, it was capable of killing instantly; with the other, it could resurrect the dead. Thus, Dagda embodied both generosity and sustenance as well as destructive force and renewal, essential attributes to the Celtic cosmic order.

If Dagda represented abundance and the power of creation, Morrigan personified the darker and more implacable aspects of existence. Known as the goddess of war, death, and sovereignty, Morrigan was a figure of great complexity and ambiguity. Often portrayed as a warrior woman with an intense presence, she also assumed the form of a black crow, a symbol of death and transformation. Her presence on the battlefields was feared and revered, as she could both inspire and protect warriors as well as presage their ruin. Morrigan was not just a goddess of destruction, but of inevitable change, the passage between cycles, and the force of nature that cannot be contained. She embodied the need for renewal through death and overcoming challenges, showing that power lies not only in creation, but also in the courage to face the unknown and accept fate.

Another central figure in the Celtic pantheon was Lugh, the god of light, arts, magic, and healing. Unlike Dagda and Morrigan, whose domains were tied to fertility and war respectively, Lugh was the master of all skills, the one who shone with the promise of creativity and improvement. Represented as a handsome and radiant young man, carrying an invincible spear and a shield that shone like the sun itself, Lugh was the patron of poets, artisans, musicians, and warriors. His role was to inspire and guide those who sought excellence, encouraging constant improvement and the pursuit of knowledge. He was also a skilled strategist and leader, often associated with the celebration of the Lughnasadh festival, which marked the beginning of the harvest and symbolized the connection between human effort and the generosity of the earth.

If Lugh represented the light of intellect and creativity, Brigid embodied the sacred warmth of home and life. As the goddess of healing, poetry, fertility, and fire, Brigid was one of the most beloved deities of the Celtic pantheon. Her image evoked protection and welcome, being invoked by women, children, and all those seeking healing and inspiration. Her dominion over fire was not only literal but also metaphorical, representing both the flame of knowledge and the warmth of the family hearth. Brigid was also a guardian of prosperity and agriculture, her presence being associated with sacred wells and healing springs. Her cult remained so ingrained in Celtic culture that, even after Christianization, she was assimilated into the figure of Saint Brigid, maintaining her influence as a protector and spiritual guide.

Finally, among the most emblematic gods was Cernunnos, the lord of the forests and animals. With an enigmatic and majestic appearance, Cernunnos was represented as a man with a serene countenance, adorned with deer antlers and often surrounded by wild creatures. He symbolized the life force of nature, the deep connection between humans and the animal world, as well as the fertility and abundance of natural cycles. His image evoked harmony between man and earth, reminding us that existence is not based solely on the domination of nature, but also on respect and integration with it. Cernunnos was invoked by hunters, travelers, and all those seeking to understand the mysteries of wildlife and cosmic balance.

In addition to these great deities, the Celtic pantheon was populated by countless local gods and goddesses, each reflecting specific aspects of the culture and environment of their tribe. These deities ranged from minor protective spirits to powerful regional gods, demonstrating the richness and diversity of Celtic thought. More than mythological figures, the Celtic gods were living expressions of the relationship between humans and the sacred, embodying the forces that shaped existence and guided those who knew how to listen to their calls.

Thus, the Celtic pantheon reflects a vibrant and interconnected worldview, where the divine is not something distant, but an essential part of the flow of life. Its multifaceted and dynamic deities not only represented the elements and cycles of nature, but also guided humans on their journey, offering protection, challenges, and teachings. By recognizing the presence of the gods on earth, in the sky, in the waters, and in their own destinies, the Celts lived in a constant dance with the sacred, understanding that every aspect of existence was permeated by invisible forces that, when honored, ensured balance and harmony of the cosmos.

Chapter 4
Ancestral Worship

The Celts' relationship with their ancestors was an indissoluble bond that transcended the barrier of death and established a bridge between the present and the past. It was believed that the spirits of the ancestors remained close, watching over their descendants and influencing the events of the world of the living. More than distant memories, the ancestors were active figures in the daily lives of the tribes, evoked for protection, guidance and strengthening of family and community identity. Respect for those who came before was a fundamental principle in Celtic society, as the wisdom accumulated by ancestors was considered essential for the harmony and continuity of the group. Thus, honoring them was not just a duty, but a vital necessity, capable of ensuring balance and prosperity.

Rituals dedicated to ancestors were performed at different times of the year, but became especially significant during the festival of Samhain, a time when the veil between worlds became thinner. During this celebration, the Celts lit bonfires and left offerings of food and drink for the spirits of their ancestors, ensuring their hospitality and recognition. It was common for families to reserve an empty place at the table for the dead, symbolizing their presence and reaffirming the bond that united them. Megalithic monuments, such as dolmens and passage tombs, also served as points of connection, being sacred places where the living could communicate with those who had departed. The belief in the continuity of the soul meant that death was not seen as an absolute end, but as a passage to another form of existence, in which family ties remained unbreakable.

In addition to physical rituals, oral tradition played an essential role in preserving ancestral memory. Bards and poets, respected figures within the Celtic social structure, were responsible for transmitting the stories of the clans, extolling the deeds of the ancestors and ensuring that their lessons were passed on. Knowledge of lineages was fundamental, as the Celts saw their ancestors not only as individuals who lived before them, but as pillars of collective identity. This strong connection to the past shaped the present and strengthened the values of the community, ensuring that each new generation carried with it the legacy of those who paved their way.

The Celts maintained the conviction that their ancestors, even after death, continued to be connected to the world of the living, exerting influence over the fate of their descendants. For them, the ancestors not only observed the journey of those who came after, but also offered protection, advice and help in times of difficulty. In return, the living had a responsibility to honor and remember their predecessors, ensuring that their memories and legacies were preserved and passed down from generation to generation. This practice was not just a symbolic gesture, but a sacred duty that ensured harmony between the two worlds and reinforced the identity and cohesion of the community.

This veneration of ancestors manifested itself in various ways, one of the most visible being the construction of tombs and megalithic monuments. These imposing structures, erected in stone, were not just burial places, but true points of contact between the living and the dead. Dolmens and passage tombs, often aligned with astronomical phenomena, served as sacred portals, allowing spiritual communication and symbolizing the continued presence of ancestors in the life of the tribe. The Celts believed that by visiting these places and paying their respects, they strengthened ties with those who had departed and ensured their benevolence for the present and future.

Offerings also played a fundamental role in this cult. Food, drink, and valuables were left in tombs and other sacred spaces as a way of showing respect and gratitude. Offerings were not only made on specific occasions, but were often integrated into daily rituals, reinforcing the belief that ancestors continued to actively participate in the lives of their descendants. In some cases, personal items of the deceased were buried with him or later delivered as tribute, reinforcing the idea of continuity between worlds. The choice of objects and food varied according to the social position and preferences of the honored ancestor, as it was believed that they could spiritually enjoy the gifts offered.

Among the many celebrations dedicated to ancestors, the festival of Samhain occupied a prominent place. During this sacred period, which marked the transition between the end of harvest and the beginning of winter, it was believed that the veil between worlds became thinner, allowing the spirits of the dead to temporarily return to the world of the living. This was a time of great reverence, in which families gathered to welcome their ancestors and ensure they were received with hospitality and respect. To do so, specific rituals were performed: bonfires were lit to illuminate the path of spirits, and tables were carefully prepared with special foods, leaving an empty place to symbolize the presence of those who had already departed. Some families reported feeling the presence of their ancestors through subtle signs – an unexpected breeze, the crackling of flames, or even vivid dreams in which they received messages and guidance.

Samhain, however, was not just a time of reunion, but also of renewal and protection. Many practices of this time aimed to ward off malevolent spirits and ensure that only benevolent ancestors approached homes. Masks and disguises were used to confuse unwanted presences, while specific rituals ensured the safety of homes and crops. The Druids, priests and spiritual guides of the Celts, played an essential role in these ceremonies, conducting sacred rites and interpreting the omens that the ancestors sent to the living.

The oral transmission of ancestral stories was another fundamental pillar of the cult of the dead. In the absence of a consolidated written tradition, bards, poets and storytellers had the mission of preserving and disseminating the memories of the clans, ensuring that the deeds of the ancestors were not forgotten. These narratives went beyond simple historical accounts – they were life lessons, founding myths, and examples of courage and wisdom that shaped collective identity. A Celtic clan was not just a group of people connected by blood, but a community united by a common heritage, and knowing its roots was essential to maintaining the cohesion and continuity of that lineage. Singing the names of ancestors and remembering their exploits was a way of making them immortal, perpetuating their legacy through the generations.

The influence of ancestors was also reflected in the social structure of the Celts. Clans and families based their identity on common lineages, reinforcing kinship ties and ensuring the transmission of knowledge, land and titles. Ancestry was a determining factor in the distribution of power and the maintenance of social order. Among warriors and leaders, knowing their genealogy was crucial to claiming positions of prestige, as lineage established not only rights, but also duties. A Celtic leader did not rule solely by his own strength and skill, but also in the name of those who came before him, carrying with him the weight of responsibility to honor and protect his people.

Furthermore, ancestor worship was deeply intertwined with the Celtic belief in the continuity of life after death. For them, death was not an absolute end, but a transition to another state of existence. The soul, eternal and indissoluble, continued its journey, being able to reincarnate, remain in the Otherworld, or act as a guide and protector of the living. This spiritual vision provided great comfort and reinforced the idea that honoring the dead was not just a tribute to the past, but a connection to the present and a bridge to the future.

Ultimately, ancestor worship was much more than just a set of religious practices – it was a foundation that supported Celtic identity. Reverence for ancestors strengthened family ties, preserved history and tradition, and offered the living a constant connection to the spiritual world. The Celts understood that they were part of a long chain of existence, in which each link depended on the other to remain strong. Honoring ancestors was, therefore, honoring oneself and ensuring that the flame of memory never went out.

For the Celts, ancestor worship was more than a sacred duty – it was the very essence of the continuity of life. Through rituals, stories and daily reverence, the living and the dead remained connected, sharing a common destiny that transcended time. Each offering left, each name remembered and each tradition preserved reinforced the belief that ancestors never truly departed, as they continued to inhabit the hearts and memories of their descendants. Thus, the Celtic lineage was perpetuated not only in blood, but in soul, ensuring that the legacy of those who came before was never lost to oblivion.

Chapter 5
Natural Cycles

Celtic existence was intrinsically aligned with natural cycles, reflecting the harmony between the elements of the Earth and cosmic movements. Time was not seen linearly, but as a continuous flow, a great spiral where birth, growth, death and rebirth intertwined in a perpetual dance. Each season carried with it a sacred teaching, an invitation to observe the changes around and within oneself. Thus, the perception of the Celtic world was based on the understanding that everything in nature has its own rhythm, an invisible pulse that governs life and death, light and darkness, abundance and scarcity. This awareness allowed each individual to live in tune with the transformations of the Earth, understanding that each phase brought with it opportunities for learning, renewal and celebration.

The Wheel of the Year symbolized this dynamic, being more than just an agricultural calendar; it was a spiritual map that guided the journey of both the individual and the collective. Through eight seasonal festivals, the Celts celebrated moments of transition and recognized the presence of the divine in every aspect of existence. The cyclical movement of the Wheel reminded us that everything in life is fleeting and that every ending brings with it a new beginning. This understanding permeated not only the way they dealt with time, but also their spirituality, their rites and their way of relating to the sacred. The balance between opposites – light and shadow, life and death, growth and retreat – was accepted as an essential part of the great universal flow, and by honoring these cycles, the Celts kept alive the connection with the forces of nature.

Each festival represented a passing point within this great cycle, a moment of introspection or celebration, as the forces of the Earth transformed. Winter brought retreat and contact with ancestors, while spring symbolized rebirth and renewal. Summer exuded vitality and celebration, and autumn marked the time of harvest and gratitude. This understanding encompassed not only the cycle of the seasons, but also the human journey – childhood, youth, maturity and old age – and existence itself as part of something greater. Thus, by following the natural cycles and honoring their phases, the Celts kept alive the sacred bond with the universe, recognizing that nature, in its wisdom, offers the path to harmony, balance and eternal renewal.

The Celtic Wheel of the Year was not limited to a simple agricultural calendar; it was a spiritual map that guided both the individual and the community through the various phases of existence. This cycle represented the eternal flow of death and rebirth, of expansion and contraction, reflecting the very dynamics of nature. Each of the eight festivals that make up this wheel marked a moment of transition, an invitation to align with the forces of the Earth and honor the cosmic cycles.

Samhain, celebrated on October 31st, was the starting point of this journey, marking the end of summer and the beginning of winter. This was the time of year when the veil between worlds became thinner, allowing communication with ancestors and contact with the Otherworld. The growing darkness invited retreat and introspection, while bonfires were lit to ward off unwanted spirits and guide those returning for a brief visit. It was a time of reverence for the dead, reflection on the past, and preparation for a new cycle of life. Many rituals involved offerings of food to the spirits, writing letters to deceased loved ones, and practicing divination to obtain guidance for the next cycle.

The transition to Yule, on December 21st, represented the longest night of the year, the winter solstice. This festival celebrated the rebirth of the Sun and the promise of new beginnings. Even at the height of darkness, there was certainty that light would return, bringing new possibilities. People decorated trees with lights and solar symbols, lit candles and bonfires, and shared community meals as a gesture of hope and renewal. Small protection rituals were common, such as burning a special log, the Yule Log, which symbolized the resistance of light against darkness.

With the gradual return of light, Imbolc arrived on February 1st, a festival dedicated to the goddess Brigid, guardian of the sacred fire, healing and inspiration. It was a time of purification and renewal, marked by the thaw and the first signs of spring. People cleaned their houses and lit candles in honor of the growing light, while making offerings to Brigid to ask for blessings of fertility and creativity. Small altars were set up with white and red flowers, milk and bread, symbols of nourishment and rebirth.

Ostara, celebrated on March 21st, marked the spring equinox, the moment of perfect balance between light and darkness. This festival symbolized fertility, flowering and the rebirth of life on Earth. It was common to plant seeds during this period, both in the soil and in symbolic aspects of life, such as new projects and intentions. Eggs, rabbits and flowers were central symbols of this celebration, representing abundance and the awakening of nature. Ritually, people painted eggs with vibrant colors and buried them in the ground as a gesture of connection with the Earth and welcoming the new season.

The peak of fertility and vital energy was celebrated in Beltane, on May 1st. This festival represented the union between masculine and feminine, the dance of life in its fullness. Bonfires were lit, and couples jumped over the flames to attract luck and blessings. The Maypole, a trunk decorated with colored ribbons, symbolized the union between heaven and earth, between the divine and the human. Dances around the mast were performed, interweaving the ribbons as a reflection of the connection between all things.

At the height of light, on June 21st, Litha took place, the summer solstice, when the Sun reached its maximum power. This was a time of celebrating abundance, energy and the coming harvest. People harvested medicinal and magical herbs, as they were believed to be at their peak energy. The bonfires of

Litha were jumped as a form of purification and strengthening, while requests were thrown into the flames to be taken to the gods.

From that point on, the days began to shorten, and on August 1st, Lughnasadh arrived, the celebration of the first harvest. This festival was dedicated to Lugh, the god of skills and arts, and represented a time of gratitude for abundance and the work done throughout the year. Breads were baked with the first harvested grains and shared among friends and family. Competitions and games were held in honor of Lugh, reinforcing community ties and the celebration of individual and collective achievements.

Finally, the cycle approached balance once again with Mabon, the autumn equinox, celebrated on September 21st. This was the time of the final harvest and recognition of the abundance of the Earth. People gave thanks for the fruits received and prepared for winter, storing food and strengthening their spiritual connections. Small rituals were performed to ensure protection and balance for the cold months ahead.

Following the Wheel of the Year was not only about honoring the natural cycles, but also understanding that life, in its essence, is made of interconnected phases. Each festival offered an opportunity for renewal, a moment of celebration and introspection, allowing the Celts to live in harmony with universal forces and recognize their connection to everything around them.

For the Celts, understanding and honoring natural cycles was more than a custom – it was a path of wisdom and belonging to the great flow of existence. Each season, each transition, reflected not only the changes of the earth, but also the internal transformations that every human being goes through throughout life. Following the Wheel of the Year meant accepting the constant movement of the universe, learning to flow with it instead of resisting. Thus, by celebrating birth and death, light and darkness, harvest and scarcity, the Celts found balance and purpose, understanding that everything, in the end, returns to the eternal cycle of creation and renewal.

Chapter 6
Celebrating Death

Darkness approaches, carrying with it echoes of the past and the whispers of ancestral spirits. The earth sleeps under a blanket of fallen leaves, and the cold announces the arrival of a new cycle. Samhain manifests not only as a change in seasons but as a portal between worlds, a sacred moment in which time dissolves and the connection with those who came before is strengthened. The Celts understood death not as an absolute end, but as an essential stage in the continuous flow of existence, an inevitable passage within the great web of life. This understanding allowed them to celebrate the transition with reverence, seeing darkness not as something to fear, but as a space for learning and renewal.

The arrival of Samhain marked a time of deep reflection and introspection. With the diminishing light and the approach of winter, nature offered a silent invitation to look inward, revisit memories, and confront inner shadows. It was a period of farewells and closures, in which old cycles were completed to make way for what was to come. The bonds with the ancestors were strengthened, as it was believed that on this night, the veil between worlds became so thin that those who had already departed could walk among the living, bringing messages, blessings, and wisdom. Respect for this presence was manifested in dedicated rituals, in feasts prepared in honor of the dead, and in symbolic gestures that ensured that their spirits were well received.

More than a festival of death, Samhain was a celebration of the eternity of the spirit and the continuity of life. The flames of sacred bonfires burned to illuminate the path of those returning, while masks were worn to confuse unwanted spirits. The symbolism of carved lanterns represented both the need for protection and the remembrance of those who were no longer physically present. This was the night when people looked to the future through divinatory practices, seeking to understand the challenges and opportunities of the new cycle. Samhain, therefore, was not just a moment of mourning or farewell, but a recognition of the interconnection between past, present, and future. By honoring the dead, the Celts reaffirmed the sacredness of existence and strengthened the certainty that, just as the earth sleeps in winter, life always finds a way to be reborn.

More than a celebration of death, Samhain represents a profound reverence for life in its totality, where death is not seen as a definitive end, but as an essential stage in the continuous cycle of existence. It is the night when the boundaries between the world of the living and the Otherworld dissolve, allowing not only communication with ancestors but also an immersion in the mysteries of existence. The veil that separates the planes becomes so thin that the spirits of those who have departed can visit the living, bringing messages, protection, and teachings that echo through the generations.

The Celts saw Samhain, celebrated on October 31st, as the point of transition between a cycle that ends and another that begins. For them, this was not only the end of the harvest but the beginning of the New Year, a time of closure and renewal. Daily activities were adjusted to accompany this change: herds were brought in from the pastures to the pens, ensuring protection against the approaching cold, and crops were carefully stored to sustain the community during the dark winter months. This period of preparation was not only practical but also laden with symbolism. Just as the earth retreated for its rest, people were invited to look within themselves, revisiting their own shadows and reflecting on the lessons of the cycle that was ending.

It was believed that during Samhain, contact with ancestors became more accessible, allowing their spirits to briefly return to the world of the living. To receive them respectfully, sacred bonfires were lit on the hilltops, whose flames served both to guide the dead back to their homes and to ward off unwanted energies that might infiltrate this opening between worlds. In addition, offerings of food and drink were left on altars or even at the doors of houses, ensuring that the spirits were well received and could share the feast with the living.

Samhain festivities were filled with rituals and customs that expressed respect for death and, at the same time, celebrated the continuity of life. Feasts were central moments of these celebrations, and food played a fundamental role in the connection between worlds. The tables were richly laden, and specific dishes were prepared for both the living and the dead. Often, a seat at the table was left empty, reserved for the visiting spirits, reinforcing the belief that they were still part of the community, even after death.

To protect themselves from malevolent entities that could also cross the veil on this night, the Celts adopted the custom of wearing masks and costumes, a practice that would transform centuries later into the costumes of modern Halloween. The idea was that by concealing their identity, the living could confuse hostile spirits, preventing them from being recognized and pursued. Furthermore, this disguise also allowed for a playful connection with the Otherworld, bringing a tone of celebration and mystery to the festivities.

Another striking aspect of Samhain was the divination rituals, considered especially powerful on this magical night. As time and space became fluid, it was believed that it was possible to glimpse the future more clearly. Various divinatory practices were performed, from observing the flames of bonfires and the way the sticks burned, to games and omens made with apples and nuts. One of the most common methods was the practice of peeling an apple continuously without breaking the peel; when thrown to the ground, the shape it assumed upon falling could indicate the initial of one's future love.

Perhaps one of the best-known customs that has survived through the centuries is that of carving faces into turnips or beets, illuminating them with candles inside. These artifacts served to illuminate the path of spirits and ward off the forces of darkness. Over time, this practice was transformed into what we know today as "Jack-o'-lantern," replacing turnips with the more abundant pumpkins in America. However, the original meaning remains: these lanterns represent the connection with the Otherworld and the remembrance of those who have departed.

Samhain was also a period of introspection, a necessary pause before the harsh winter. As the days grew shorter and the darkness lingered, the Celts understood that this was the time to look inward and reflect on the lessons of the past year. Just as nature entered a state of dormancy, the human spirit also needed this retreat to strengthen itself. This was the time to leave behind what no longer served, to end cycles, and to prepare the way for the new beginnings that would come with spring.

Samhain, therefore, was not just a festival of death, but a celebration of the eternal cycle of existence. Through connection with ancestors, honor paid to the dead, and reflection on the impermanence of life, the Celts reaffirmed their faith in the continuity of the soul and the certainty that, even in the darkest nights, light would always find a way back.

By celebrating Samhain today, we can reclaim this ancestral wisdom, honoring those who came before us and recognizing the importance of each phase of life. We can light candles in honor of our loved ones who have departed, prepare a symbolic meal for them, or simply take a moment to reflect on our own journey. Thus, we keep alive the flame of this ancient tradition, remembering that death is not an end, but a portal to renewal.

Samhain teaches us that death and life are not opposites, but inseparable parts of the same sacred cycle. By looking to the past and connecting with those who came before us, we also prepare for what is to come, carrying with us the wisdom of those who have departed. In this moment of transition, the veil between worlds dissolves not only to remind us of the presence of spirits, but also to invite us to accept our own shadows, to end what needs to be left behind, and to walk with more awareness towards the future. And so, between light and darkness, farewell and rebirth, Samhain lives on, traversing the centuries as a reminder that nothing is truly lost—everything is transformed.

Chapter 7
Rebirth of the Sun

The silence of winter covers the earth like a sacred mantle, while the longest night of the year looms on the horizon. Cold dominates the dormant fields, and darkness seems to reign supreme, but at the heart of this somber period, a promise is renewed: the return of light. Yule, the winter solstice, is not just an astronomical marker; it is a moment of profound transformation, in which darkness reaches its peak and then gives way to the slow awakening of the Sun. For the Celts, this event symbolized the rebirth of life, the victory of light over shadow, and the certainty that, however harsh the winter, the wheel of time would continue to turn. Yule night was a reminder that light never completely disappears, it only withdraws to re-emerge with renewed vigor in due time.

Faced with this cosmic renewal, the Celts performed rituals that reflected their deep connection with nature and the cycles of the Earth. Fire, a symbol of life force and the rising Sun, occupied a central role in the celebrations. Bonfires were lit to greet the return of light, while candles illuminated homes, warding off darkness and attracting good energies for the new cycle that was beginning. The Yule log, a large piece of wood specially chosen to be burned during the festive night, represented the closing of a cycle and the fertilization of the soil for the future. Its ashes were kept as talismans of protection and renewal, ensuring the continuity of life and prosperity throughout the year. In addition, evergreen trees, such as pines and hollies, were revered as symbols of immortality and resistance, as they remained green even in the coldest months, reaffirming the presence of life amidst the apparent dormancy of nature.

The celebration of Yule was also a time of introspection, an invitation to look inward and recognize one's own inner light. Just as the Sun slowly returned to the sky, bringing warmth and hope, the Celts believed that this renewing energy could be cultivated within each being. This period was conducive to reflections on the year that was ending, for gratitude and for setting new intentions for the future. The rebirth of the Sun mirrored the rebirth of the soul, encouraging each individual to abandon what no longer served them and prepare for what was to come. In this way, Yule was not just a festival of external celebration, but also an internal rite of passage, a time to recognize that no matter how long the night, dawn always arrives, bringing with it new possibilities, growth, and renewal.

Celebrated on December 21st, Yule marks the turning point of winter, when darkness reaches its peak and light begins to return. More than just an astronomical event, this date represents the birth of the Sun god, who emerges from the womb of the Great Mother to begin his upward journey across the sky.

With him, the promise of warmth, fertility, and new life is reborn. For the ancient Celtic and Germanic peoples, this moment symbolized the renewal of the cycle of nature and the certainty that, even in the darkest of times, light never completely disappears—it simply awaits the right moment to re-emerge with renewed strength.

Yule celebrations were marked by deeply symbolic rituals aimed at honoring the Sun and celebrating the return of light. Sacred bonfires were lit, not only to warm bodies chilled by winter, but to illuminate souls and strengthen the bond between men and gods. The fire, which consumed the wood and danced in golden flames, represented the reborn Sun and the life force that was renewed. Meanwhile, in homes, candles were lit in every corner, warding off darkness and inviting good energies for the new cycle that was beginning.

One of the most significant customs of this festival was the decoration of trees with lights and ornaments. Evergreen trees, such as pine and fir, were seen as symbols of immortality and resistance because they remained green even in the harshest months. They were adorned with dried fruits, ribbons, bells, and small talismans that represented wishes for prosperity and health for the coming year. Each ornament carried a special meaning: the fruits symbolized abundance, the candles referred to light and protection, and the bells were used to ward off unwanted spirits and bring good vibes to the home. This ancestral custom would later be assimilated by different cultures and give rise to the tradition of the Christmas tree.

Banquets also played an essential role in Yule celebrations. Families and communities gathered around laden tables, sharing food and toasting to the abundance of the earth. Traditional dishes were prepared with ingredients that referred to fertility and the cycle of life. Roasted meats, aromatic breads, dried fruits, and hot drinks, such as mead and wine spiced with spices, were served as a way of giving thanks for the blessings received and as a request for abundance for the following months. Food not only nourished the body but also strengthened the bonds between people, reaffirming the importance of unity and sharing in times of cold and introspection.

Among the many symbols of Yule, one of the most important was the Yule log. Carefully chosen, this large piece of wood was burned at the center of the festivities, in a ritual laden with meaning. It represented the old year that was ending and, as it was consumed by the flames, it symbolized the renewal of life and the arrival of a new cycle. Its ashes were carefully collected and kept as protective amulets, used to fertilize the land and ensure good harvests in the future. Some families kept a piece of the burned log to light the fire of the next Yule, symbolizing the continuity of life and the connection between the past, present, and future.

But Yule was not just a time for external festivities; it also invited introspection and retreat. In the cold and dark days of winter, the Celts turned inward, contemplating the mysteries of life and death. It was a period of reflection, of evaluating the ending year and preparing for what was to come. Many performed silent candlelight rituals, writing on scrolls or pieces of wood what they wanted to leave behind. These messages were then burned in the sacred fire, as a symbolic act of release and transformation. It was a time to purify the soul, renew hopes, and strengthen the connection with ancestors and nature spirits.

Furthermore, ancient peoples believed that during Yule, the veil between worlds became thinner, allowing for closer contact with spiritual beings. Therefore, many magical practices were performed during this period. Amulets were made and consecrated to fire, herbs were burned for purification, and offerings were left in the forest as a way of thanking and respecting the spirits of the earth. Among the most used herbs were mistletoe and holly, plants associated with protection, love, and fertility. Mistletoe, in particular, was considered sacred because it grew on the branches of trees without touching the ground, being seen as a gift from the gods.

In short, Yule was a festival of light and rebirth, a reminder that no matter how deep the darkness, light always returns. The celebration of this natural cycle reaffirmed the hope and resilience of the human spirit, showing that even the most difficult times are fleeting and that there is always the promise of a new dawn. Today, as we celebrate Yule, we can reclaim this ancestral wisdom and apply it to our own lives. We can light candles to symbolize our inner light, decorate our homes with sprigs of pine and holly to attract protection and abundance, and set aside time for reflection and renewal. Thus, we honor not only the cycle of nature but also our own cycle of growth and transformation.

Yule teaches us that even on the longest and coldest nights, the promise of rebirth remains alive, waiting for the right moment to bloom. The light that returns to the world is not only that of the Sun, but also the inner flame that guides and strengthens us. By aligning ourselves with this sacred cycle, we recognize that each winter brings with it the seed of renewal and that, just as nature awakens to a new cycle, we too are invited to be reborn, leaving behind what no longer serves us and embracing the future with hope and wisdom.

Chapter 8
Purification and Renewal

The long stillness of winter begins to dissolve, and a whisper of life runs through the dormant earth. The first rays of sunlight stretch their golden fingers over fields still covered in ice, while small buds dare to break through the cold soil, announcing the arrival of a new cycle. Imbolc is the time when nature slowly awakens, stretching after the deep sleep of winter, and the promise of spring begins to manifest in a subtle but irresistible way. The darkness of winter gives way to the growing light, and the energy of renewal pulsates in the earth and in the hearts of those who observe it. The Celts understood this transition not only as a natural phenomenon, but as a reflection of their own inner rebirth, an invitation to purify, renew, and prepare for the coming times of growth and abundance.

Dedicated to the goddess Brigid, Imbolc was celebrated as a festival of light, purification, and inspiration. Brigid, the deity of sacred fire, healing, and poetry, symbolized the flame of creativity and renewal, guiding those who sought clarity and transformation. Her aspects as healer and guardian of the home made this period a propitious time for spiritual and physical cleansing, eliminating the impurities of winter and making space for the new. Houses were swept and purified with sacred herbs, while candles were lit to illuminate the paths and invoke protection and blessings. The flame of Imbolc was not only that of physical fire, but also that of inspiration that warms the soul and ignites the desires for growth and fulfillment.

In addition to purification rituals, this festival was a time of observation and preparation. The signs of nature were carefully interpreted, as it was believed that they revealed clues about what was to come. The practice of divination gained strength, reflecting the search for understanding the cycles of life and the choices to be made in the following months. The symbolism of water was also present, representing fluidity, cleansing, and rebirth, being used in rites of purification and renewal. Thus, Imbolc not only marked the awakening of the earth, but also encouraged each individual to awaken to their own possibilities. It was a call to release what no longer served, to embrace the light of knowledge and intuition, and to prepare the spirit for the fertile times to come.

Celebrated on February 1st, Imbolc marks the midpoint between the winter solstice and the spring equinox, a period of transition in which the earth, still enveloped by the remnants of cold, begins to reveal the first signs of rebirth. Small buds break through the soil hardened by winter, announcing the promise of returning life. The sunlight, increasingly present, spreads its brilliance over the dormant fields, and the singing of birds, returning to their nests, echoes like a hymn of renewal. This awakening of nature also reflects an invitation to inner rebirth, a call to cleanse what no longer serves and prepare the spirit for the new cycles that are approaching.

Imbolc is dedicated to the goddess Brigid, one of the most beloved deities of the Celtic pantheon. Guardian of the sacred fire, healing, poetry, and inspiration, Brigid represents the life force that renews itself and the creative power that drives all life forms. Her fire not only warms homes and purifies energies, but also symbolizes the spark of creativity, the illumination of the mind, and the hope that burns in our hearts. During this festival, the Celts honored Brigid with rituals that sought to attract her protection and blessings, ensuring that her sacred flame continued to shine in both the physical and spiritual worlds.

Imbolc celebrations were marked by rituals and customs aimed at purifying and renewing energies. It was tradition to clean houses and decorate them with flowers and green branches, bringing to the environment the promise of spring and the freshness of the approaching new season. Sacred bonfires were lit in honor of Brigid, and candles illuminated every room of the home, representing the growing light of the sun and the divine protection of the goddess. The flame of these candles symbolized the warmth needed to awaken the earth and renew the spirit, warding off any darkness remaining from the cold months.

One of the most emblematic customs of Imbolc was the making of the Brigid's Cross, a solar symbol made of straw or reed that represented the goddess and her protection. These crosses were carefully intertwined and placed in strategic locations such as doors, windows, stables and fields, with the intention of attracting luck, health and prosperity. The act of weaving the cross was not just a symbolic gesture, but a moment of connection with Brigid, an invocation of her presence and her blessings for the home and family. Each intertwined thread carried the intention of renewal and protection, making the cross a sacred amulet for the year that was beginning.

Another fundamental aspect of Imbolc celebrations was purification with water, an element that symbolized the cleansing of stagnant winter energies and preparation for the new cycle. The Celts performed ritual baths in rivers and springs, believing that the water from these sources possessed healing and purifying properties. In addition, water was used to clean houses and sacred objects, eliminating impurities accumulated during the months of darkness. This ritual not only renewed physical spaces, but also promoted a deep process of spiritual cleansing, allowing each individual to free themselves from the past and open themselves to the new opportunities that spring would bring.

Imbolc was also a propitious period for divination and prediction of the future. The Celts believed that, at this time of year, the veil between the worlds became thinner, facilitating communication with spirits and obtaining insights about what was to come. Divination rituals were widely practiced, using methods such as bone reading, dream interpretation, and observation of the signs of nature. Every little detail was carefully analyzed, as it was believed that the earth and the elements offered valuable clues about the challenges and blessings of the new cycle.

Thus, Imbolc was more than a festival of transition between seasons; it was a sacred time of introspection, renewal, and preparation for the future. The celebration of the goddess Brigid and the performance of purification rituals allowed each individual to align with the rhythms of nature, releasing what no longer served a purpose and embracing the light of knowledge and intuition. It was a time of hope, of opening arms to the abundance that was to come and of reaffirming the commitment to one's own growth and well-being.

As we celebrate Imbolc today, we can rescue this ancestral wisdom and incorporate it into our lives in a meaningful way. We can light candles to symbolize the renewal of light, perform energy cleansing in our homes, take purifying baths, and set new intentions for the coming months. Honoring the goddess Brigid does not only mean following ancient rituals, but also allowing her sacred flame to shine within us, inspiring us to grow, create, and transform ourselves along with the cycles of nature.

Imbolc reminds us that all renewal begins within, in the subtle space where old shadows are dissolved to give way to light. Just as the earth awakens from its winter sleep, we are invited to open our eyes to our own transformations, allowing the flame of inspiration and clarity to illuminate our paths. Purification is not just a symbolic act, but a process of liberation and preparation for the cycles to come. And, by embracing this energy of renewal, we reaffirm our connection to the flow of life, trusting that every winter brings with it the promise of a new spring.

Chapter 9
Spring Equinox

The awakening of spring brings with it an explosion of colors, aromas, and renewed energy. The cold of winter dissipates, giving way to the mild warmth of the Sun, which now shines more intensely over fields that bloom and rivers that flow freely again. Ostara marks this moment of balance and renewal, the sacred instant in which light and darkness meet in perfect harmony, dividing day and night into equal parts. Nature opens up in celebration, and with it, everything that has been dormant awakens, inviting men and women to celebrate life in its fullness. For the Celts, this period symbolized not only the fertility of the earth, but also the opportunity to sow new intentions, nurture dreams, and strengthen the connection with the infinite cycle of existence. Spring arrived as a reminder that life always finds a way to be reborn.

Ostara was a festival of joy, gratitude, and hope, reflecting the triumph of light over shadows. The energy of this equinox impelled the Celts to plant seeds, both in the soil and in their own hearts, trusting that time would bring growth and abundance. The rituals of this period were dedicated to the forces of fertility and rebirth, evoking the blessing of the earth and the deities to ensure good harvests and prosperity. The symbolism of the egg, present in the festivities, represented the infinite potential of creation, the promise of what was yet to come. Likewise, the rabbit, with its extraordinary capacity for multiplication, was seen as a messenger of vitality and the renewal of life, reinforcing the idea that spring was a time of expansion and abundance.

The arrival of Ostara was also an invitation to celebrate balance, both in the natural world and in the inner journey of each individual. Just as the Earth found a moment of equality between light and darkness, the Celts understood that this was a propitious period to reflect on their own lives and seek harmony between their desires, challenges, and achievements. Spring taught that every ending brings a new beginning and that, by honoring the cycles of nature, it was possible to align oneself with the flow of the universe. Thus, Ostara was not just a festival of colors and rituals, but a call to embrace renewal, awaken creativity, and trust in the transformative power of life, which always finds a way to flourish, regardless of the harshness of the winter that came before.

Celebrated on March 21st, Ostara marks a sacred instant of balance, in which day and night share the same duration, representing the harmony between opposing forces that govern the universe. At this moment, the Sun, on its ascending journey, crosses the celestial equator, bringing with it the dawn of a new season. With it come longer days, mild temperatures, and the vibrant awakening of nature, which is adorned with colors, scents, and renewed life. The earth, once silent under the cold of winter, now opens to receive the energy of rebirth, inviting everyone to celebrate this period of transformation and growth.

Ostara is a festival of joy and hope, a tribute to the triumph of life over death, of light over darkness. It is the time to plant seeds, both in the fertile soil and in the soul, to nurture dreams and intentions, and to open oneself to the infinite possibilities that spring brings. Just as plants break through the earth in search of the Sun, we are called to flourish, expanding our horizons and embracing renewal with confidence and gratitude.

Ostara celebrations were filled with rituals and customs that honored the fertility of the earth and celebrated the rebirth of nature. Among the most striking symbols was the egg, the ultimate representation of creative potential and the promise of new life. These eggs were carefully decorated with vibrant colors and symbolic drawings, which varied according to the traditions and intentions of each community. Red, to attract strength and vitality; green, to evoke fertility and connection to the earth; gold, to invoke prosperity and abundance. At the end of the festivities, these eggs were offered as good luck charms or buried in the fields to bless the crops that were to come.

Another fundamental symbol of Ostara is the rabbit, an animal associated with fertility and abundance. Its impressive reproductive capacity made it a messenger of renewal and the incessant cycle of life. It was common for communities to observe the behavior of rabbits in nature as an omen for the following seasons, interpreting their movements and habits as signs of what was to come. Over time, this symbolism intertwined with other traditions, giving rise to the figure of the Easter bunny, the one who brings colorful eggs as gifts, perpetuating an ancestral custom that dates back to immemorial times.

Preparation for Ostara included decorating houses and altars with freshly picked flowers and green branches, symbols of the rebirth of nature and the ephemeral beauty of spring. People brought into their homes elements that evoked the vibrant energy of the season, creating environments that reflected the celebration of life in its fullness. Small arrangements of lavender, daisies, and lilies were placed on tables and windows, while garlands made of ivy and willow adorned doors, inviting the renewing energy of the season to enter.

Ostara banquets were plentiful and colorful, filled with fresh, seasonal foods that extolled the bounty of the earth. Freshly baked breads, honey cakes, cheeses, juicy fruits, and freshly picked vegetables were served, along with beverages made from aromatic herbs and wildflowers. A traditional recipe that used to mark this celebration was Ostara bread, prepared with ingredients that symbolized fertility and renewal. To make it, they mixed:
- 3 cups of wheat flour
- 1 teaspoon of salt
- 2 tablespoons of honey
- 1 tablespoon of dry yeast
- 1 cup of warm milk
- 1 tablespoon of melted butter

- 1 egg
- Herbs and seeds to taste (such as rosemary, fennel or poppy seeds)

The preparation consisted of dissolving the yeast in the warm milk together with the honey, letting the mixture rest until foamy. Then, the dry ingredients were combined, and the liquid mixture was added little by little, forming a soft and elastic dough. After kneading, the dough rested until it doubled in size. Then, small loaves were shaped, which were baked until they acquired a golden crust and an irresistible aroma. This bread, in addition to being a symbol of fertility, was shared among the participants as a gesture of union and prosperity.

In addition to culinary festivities, Ostara was a propitious time for fertility and renewal rituals. A traditional custom involved intentional sowing, where people planted seeds while visualizing wishes and purposes for the new cycle. Each seed thrown into the ground represented a goal, and the responsibility of caring for the plant symbolized the commitment to nurture these dreams until they blossomed. Some traditions also included the practice of ritual baths in streams or natural springs, purifying body and spirit to receive the blessings of spring.

Offerings were made to the deities of earth and fertility, such as Eostre, the goddess associated with the rebirth of spring. These offerings could include grains, fruits, flowers, or even small breads and cakes, which were left in groves or near ancient trees, as a way of gratitude and connection with natural forces. Fire also played an important role in Ostara rituals, with candles lit in shades of yellow and green to symbolize the growing light of the Sun and the renewing energy of the earth.

In essence, Ostara is a festival that celebrates balance, fertility, and rebirth. It is an opportunity to honor the life force that awakens with spring, to contemplate the beauty of nature, and to open oneself to new possibilities. Just as the Earth renews itself, we too can reinvent ourselves, leaving behind what no longer serves us and embracing with enthusiasm the paths that lie ahead.

As we celebrate Ostara today, we can rescue this ancestral wisdom and apply it in our own lives. Creating symbolic rituals, planting new intentions, and celebrating the abundance that surrounds us are ways of connecting with natural cycles and the energy of renewal that this season offers us. Whether through small gestures or elaborate rituals, the important thing is to honor spring not only as a season of the year, but as a constant invitation to transformation and personal flourishing.

Ostara reminds us that life is a constant flow of renewal and growth, a cycle where each ending brings with it the promise of a new beginning. Just as the earth flourishes after the dormancy of winter, we too are called to awaken, to plant our intentions with confidence, and to nurture our dreams with patience and dedication. The balance between light and darkness teaches us that all phases of the journey have their purpose, and that, by aligning ourselves with the rhythms of nature, we find the strength to flourish. May this season inspire us to embrace rebirth with joy, allowing spring to happen not only around us, but also within us.

Chapter 10
Fire and Fertility

The earth radiates its vital energy, renewed by the growing heat that awakens each dormant seed and makes the fields bloom in a vibrant spectacle of colors and aromas. The natural cycle reaches its peak, and fertility spreads in all forms of life, reflecting the perfect balance between heaven and earth. Beltane, the Celtic celebration that marks this moment of exuberance and transition, shines with the intense glow of sacred bonfires and the collective joy that echoes in dance, rituals, and the union of bodies and spirits. Ancient peoples recognized this date as a sacred moment, where the primordial energy of creation manifested itself with force, opening paths for blessings, protection, and renewal. It was not just a festival to celebrate spring, but a call to connect with the elemental forces that govern life, allowing each individual to align themselves with the natural rhythms of the universe.

Fire, the central element of Beltane, symbolizes both passion and purification, representing the spark of life that burns in the heart of nature and human beings. The crackling flames illuminate the darkness and strengthen the bonds between the participants, creating an atmosphere of ecstasy and communion. During this special night, vibrant dances and chants echo through the hills, and the light of the bonfires mixes with the brilliance of the stars, connecting the earthly world to the sacred. In this enchanted setting, the veil between worlds becomes thinner, allowing contact with mystical beings and with the very divine essence that inhabits each being. It is a time of magic and possibilities, in which the energy of the earth pulsates intensely, ready to be directed to creation and abundance. The natural cycle teaches that this is the time to plant not only in fertile soil but also in the soul, cultivating desires, intentions, and dreams that will flourish throughout the year.

Beltane also exalts the duality and harmony of opposites, celebrating the union between the masculine and feminine principles, which transcends the physical body and manifests as the creative force of the universe. This sacred fusion is represented in ancient Celtic myths by the union of the God and the Goddess, whose cosmic dance fertilizes the earth and ensures the continuity of life. The rituals of this period honor this vital energy, from jumping over bonfires, which symbolize purification and the courage to go through new cycles, to the erection of the maypole, which represents the axis of the world and the union of the elements. Each gesture, each chant, and each offering made during Beltane has a deep meaning, rooted in the ancestral wisdom that understood the interdependence between man and nature. This understanding is still reflected in the community bonds that are strengthened in the celebration, as the energy of fertility is not limited to the physical field, but expands to all areas of existence. It is an invitation to renewal, to the awakening of the senses, and to the recognition of the creative power that inhabits each being.

Celebrated on May 1st, Beltane marks the height of spring, when nature reveals its fullness, overflowing in a spectacle of vibrant colors and intoxicating fragrances. Each flower that blooms, each fruit that forms, and each being that awakens to life carries the promise of abundance and renewal. In this sacred moment, the fire of passion is lit not only on earth but also in hearts, reflecting the primordial union between the God and the Goddess, the divine principles that govern creation and sustain the balance of the world. More than just a festival, Beltane is a portal to the vital energy that permeates all forms of existence, an invitation to celebrate, dance, and surrender to the creative force that pulsates in each being.

For the Celts, Beltane represented not only the transition of the seasons but also the beginning of the summer season, a period of expansion, fertility, and connection with the rhythms of the earth. The arrival of this new phase was greeted with vibrant rituals that reinforced community and spiritual bonds. The cattle, essential for subsistence, were taken to pasture under the protection of the gods, and to ensure their health and prosperity, one of the oldest and most symbolic rituals of the celebration was performed: the passage of the animals between two large bonfires. It was believed that smoke and flames had purifying and protective power, warding off diseases and misfortunes throughout the cycle that was beginning. This same principle of purification applied to people, who jumped over sacred bonfires in search of renewal, courage, and blessings for the journey ahead. Each crackling flame carried with it fears and uncertainties, transforming them into strength and vitality.

The Beltane bonfires, erected on the hills and in the centers of the villages, were not only sources of light and heat but manifestations of the divine fire itself that permeates creation. Around them, the community gathered to celebrate the fertility of the earth, dancing and chanting songs that evoked the harmony between the elements and the coming abundance. Between rhythmic steps and laughter, the boundaries between the physical and spiritual world became thinner, allowing magic to flow freely. It was a time when the gods walked among mortals, when the energies of the earth and the cosmos intertwined in perfect communion.

Another striking symbol of Beltane was the erection of the maypole, a large tree trunk adorned with colorful ribbons, flowers, and garlands. The mast represented the axis of the world, the sacred link between heaven and earth, and its symbolism went beyond mere ornamentation. It embodied the fusion of masculine and feminine principles, complementary forces that, in harmony, ensured the continuity of life. The dances around the mast, with ribbons intertwined in circular movements, represented the intertwining of creative energies, the celebration of fertility in its purest essence. Young and old participated in this ritual, weaving with their steps and gestures the manifestation of universal balance.

Beltane was also a propitious period for rituals of love and fertility. Couples who wished to strengthen their union or attract passion shared moments under the light of the bonfires, dancing together and often jumping over the flames hand in hand. This act symbolized not only mutual commitment but also the willingness to face challenges and grow side by side. In addition, offerings were left in the woods and at natural altars in honor of the deities of fertility, such as the goddess Brigid and the god Cernunnos, guardians of abundance and life. Small bundles of herbs, honey, milk, and flowers were deposited with gratitude, sealing requests for protection and prosperity for homes, fields, and hearts.

During this magical night, nature seemed to vibrate in tune with the desires and intentions of those who surrendered to the flow of celebration. It was said that portals between worlds opened, allowing communication with earth spirits and enchanted beings. The whispers of the wind carried hidden messages, and those who knew how to listen could glimpse the future or receive valuable guidance. The dew of the following morning, carefully collected, was considered an elixir of beauty and youth, a gift from the earth itself to those who honored it with respect and devotion.

Beltane, in its essence, is a celebration of the vigor of life, the passion that drives creation, and the magic that permeates each being. By connecting with this ancestral tradition, we open space for the energy of abundance and renewal in our own journeys. Whether through dance, fire, or simple gestures of gratitude, we can rescue the wisdom of the ancients and apply it to our daily lives. Beltane teaches us that fertility goes beyond the earth; it manifests itself in the ideas we cultivate, the relationships we nurture, and the dreams we dare to plant. It is a time of surrender, joy, and celebration of life in its fullness.

Beltane invites us to surrender to the flow of life, to warm ourselves in the flame of passion, and to trust in the fertility of our dreams. Just as the earth flourishes in abundance, we are called to expand our own limits, cultivate intentions, and dance with the vibrant energy of creation. May the light of ancestral bonfires continue to shine within us, illuminating our paths and reminding us that life, in its essence, is an eternal invitation to celebration and renewal.

Chapter 11
Summer Solstice

The sun shines with maximum intensity, pouring its vibrant light over green fields, lush forests, and crystal clear waters. The earth responds to this solar abundance with exuberance, offering ripe fruits, herbs laden with power, and flowers in full bloom. The Summer Solstice, known as Litha, marks this apex of light, a moment of splendor and vitality in which solar energy reaches its peak, impregnating nature and human beings with strength, warmth, and expansion. The longest day of the year celebrates the connection between humanity and the Sun, the primary source of life, energy, and growth. Since time immemorial, ancient peoples have understood this cycle as a sacred moment of gratitude and celebration, a period in which the visible and spiritual worlds intertwine, allowing the manifestation of intentions, blessings, and transformation.

Litha is a time of power, marked by the exuberance of life and the radiant force of solar fire. In various traditions, rituals were conducted to honor the Sun, channel its energy, and ensure fertility, prosperity, and protection. At the heart of the celebrations, sacred bonfires burned on hills and fields, reflecting the celestial flame itself that warms and sustains existence. These bonfires not only illuminated the night but symbolized the connection with the divine, purifying energies, renewing purposes, and strengthening the bond between earth and sky. During this period, it was believed that harvested herbs and plants had amplified power, being used for cures, spells, and amulets. The sun's rays, so intense on this day, were seen as conductors of vitality and protection, capable of impregnating bodies, houses, and crops with their beneficial force. It was also a time of fullness and celebration of fertility, as the earth, at the height of its productivity, mirrored the generosity of sunlight.

The expansive energy of Litha invites the manifestation of dreams and desires, taking advantage of the peak of solar strength to propel projects, transform intentions into reality, and celebrate life in its entirety. The ancients knew that, just as the Sun reaches its zenith and then begins its journey of decline, this moment of splendor is also a reminder of the impermanence of natural cycles. The balance between light and shadow, expansion and retreat, is present in every aspect of existence. Therefore, Litha not only exalts the brilliance of the Sun but also teaches the wisdom of recognizing the rhythms of nature and learning to flow with them. It is an invitation to connect with this vibrant energy, absorbing its strength to nourish body, mind, and spirit, strengthening bonds with the earth, with the community, and with one's own life purpose.

Celebrated on June 21st, Litha marks the culmination of the solar journey when the Sun reaches its zenith and the light extends longer, enveloping the earth in warmth and vitality. At this time of year, nature reveals all its splendor, displaying vibrantly colored flowers, succulent fruits, and green fields that reflect the fullness of the season. The Summer Solstice is an invitation to celebrate life and abundance, a moment in which the brilliance of the Sun manifests itself at its maximum power, nourishing everything around it with energy and growth.

For the Celts, Litha was a festival of extreme importance, full of rituals and customs aimed at honoring the Sun and the generosity of the earth. The hills were illuminated by sacred bonfires, erected in homage to the celestial fire, whose heat was considered essential for the fertility and prosperity of the land and its people. The burning flame of the bonfires not only represented the strength of the Sun but also functioned as a channel of purification and spiritual renewal. People danced around the fire, absorbing its vitality and strengthening their connection with the forces of nature, in a symbolic act of celebrating life and the transformative power of light.

Among the many customs practiced at this festival, the harvesting of magical herbs played a central role. It was believed that plants harvested during Litha were imbued with a special power, enhanced by the intensity of sunlight. Herbs such as mugwort, St. John's wort, lavender, and rosemary were carefully collected before sunrise and used to make amulets, potions, and incenses. These preparations were used in rituals of healing, protection, and prosperity, being saved for use throughout the year. In addition, hanging branches of these herbs on the doors and windows of houses was a common custom, as it was believed that they ward off negative energies and bring blessings to the home.

Litha was also a propitious time for performing solar magic rituals, in which the ancients sought to channel the energy of the Sun to manifest their dreams and achieve their goals. Prosperity rituals were quite popular, taking advantage of the expansive power of the Sun to attract abundance and growth. To do this, small spells were performed, such as lighting golden or yellow candles, symbolizing sunlight, and reciting intentions of abundance and success. Gold objects and sunstones, such as citrine and tiger's eye, were used in these rituals to amplify the energy of manifestation.

Healing rituals were also of great importance, as sunlight was seen as a source of vitality and restoration. Herbal baths were prepared under the midday sun, in which leaves and flowers of medicinal plants were immersed in warm water, creating a solar elixir capable of invigorating the body and spirit. In addition, it was common to drink infusions made with herbs harvested during the solstice, believing that these potions strengthened health and balanced emotions.

The protective energy of the Sun was also invoked during Litha, mainly through the creation of solar amulets. Small discs of wood or clay were engraved with solar symbols and consecrated to fire, later being carried as talismans to ensure protection and courage. Another traditional custom was the burning of requests and intentions in sacred bonfires. People wrote their wishes on pieces of paper or dried leaves and threw them into the flames, trusting that the fire would carry their intentions to the gods and benevolent spirits.

In addition to rituals and spells, Litha celebrations included outdoor feasts, in which the abundance of the season was celebrated with tables laden with fresh fruits, vegetables, and freshly harvested grains. Yellow and golden foods, such as corn, honey, and peaches, were especially appreciated as they symbolized solar energy. Honey cakes and breads decorated with seeds were also prepared, being shared among friends and family amid songs, dances, and stories told by the firelight.

The celebrations extended until dawn, as it was believed that the night of the solstice was magical, a period in which the veil between worlds was thinner, allowing contact with nature spirits and enchanted beings. It was a propitious time to leave offerings to elementals, such as fairies and elves, in gratitude for the fertility of the earth. Small pieces of bread, honey, and milk were left in gardens and woods as gifts for these beings, ensuring their protection and good harvests in the future.

Litha, therefore, is more than a festival of light; it is a time of deep connection with solar energy, the abundance of the earth, and the flow of natural cycles. To celebrate it is to honor life in its fullness, to recognize the generosity of nature, and to take advantage of this period of maximum vitality to drive dreams and purposes. By aligning ourselves with this powerful energy, we can absorb its strength to illuminate our paths, renew our intentions, and strengthen ourselves for the challenges to come.

Thus, as the Summer Solstice draws its brilliance at the apex of the sky and slowly begins its return journey, we are reminded that all brilliance carries within itself the seed of transformation. Litha is not just a tribute to light, but an invitation to be aware of the cycles that govern existence, to celebrate fullness without losing sight of the transience of life. May the energy of this moment inspire courage to expand, wisdom to recognize the time of retreat, and gratitude to honor the gift of light that warms, nourishes, and guides us.

Chapter 12
First Harvest

The earth responds to the cycle of life with generosity, offering its first fruits in an outburst of abundance and gratitude. The golden wheat fields shine under the sunlight, and the aroma of freshly baked bread fills the air, announcing the arrival of Lughnasadh, the Celtic festival that marks the beginning of the harvest. This is a time of acknowledgment for the effort dedicated to cultivation, a celebration of the balance between human labor and natural gifts. Each ear of grain, each ripe fruit, and each harvested bundle symbolize not only physical abundance but also the realization of individual and collective efforts, strengthening the bonds between the community and the land. The cycle of planting and harvesting reflects the very flow of life, teaching that everything requires patience, dedication, and respect for natural rhythms. Lughnasadh invites gratitude, recognition of the blessings received, and the sharing of prosperity as a way of honoring the interdependence between human beings and nature.

The festival is named after Lugh, the god of light, skill, and strategic intelligence, whose qualities were fundamental to the success of the harvest and overcoming challenges. At its core, Lughnasadh celebrates not only material abundance but also the enhancement of human capabilities, the courage to face difficulties, and the importance of community unity. The ancient Celts held competitions of strength and skill in honor of Lugh, symbolizing the merit of effort and the reward for hard work. These trials, which included races, fights, and physical challenges, were a way to reaffirm the resilient spirit of the community and prepare for the times to come. More than a festival of abundance, Lughnasadh was a time for learning and recognizing one's achievements, a reminder that the harvest is not restricted to the fields, but also to personal growth, relationships, and dreams cultivated over time.

As the grains are harvested and stored, there is also an awareness that a cycle is coming to an end, opening space for reflections on the future. The summer heat begins to show signs of its farewell, and the promise of autumn hints on the horizon. Lughnasadh is, therefore, a point of transition, an invitation to introspection about the fruits harvested not only on the land but also in the journey of each individual. The celebration of the harvest is intertwined with the recognition of the impermanence of cycles, teaching that prosperity must be appreciated with gratitude, but also with wisdom. The sharing of food and fruits symbolizes the awareness that abundance is strengthened when shared, creating deeper bonds between members of the community. Thus, honoring Lughnasadh is not only celebrating what has been achieved but preparing for the challenges and opportunities that the next cycle will bring, keeping the spirit of work, unity, and gratitude always alive.

Celebrated on August 1st, Lughnasadh represents a significant milestone in the Celtic calendar, a time when the harvest begins to be gathered, and the hard work of planting and cultivating finally translates into tangible fruits. The festival is an occasion for gratitude, an acknowledgment of both the effort dedicated to the land and the generosity of nature, which rewards with abundance those who dedicate themselves to it with respect. More than a mere agricultural event, Lughnasadh symbolizes the interdependence between human labor and natural forces, a sacred link that sustains life and nourishes the spirit of the community.

The festival is dedicated to the god Lugh, master of all skills, lord of light, art, and war. His figure personifies strength, strategic intelligence, and dexterity, qualities essential for both the success of the harvest and overcoming daily challenges. Lugh was not just an agricultural god, but a symbol of personal improvement and overcoming. Just as the harvest requires preparation, knowledge, and patience, life demands effort and continuous learning. Therefore, during Lughnasadh, celebrations went beyond simply giving thanks for the harvested grains and fruits, also promoting the appreciation of human capabilities and the recognition of individual and collective talents.

The festivities were marked by rituals and customs that reinforced the connection between the people and the gods, expressing gratitude for the harvest and ensuring the continuity of abundance. The ancient

Celts believed that offering the first grains and fruits to the gods was a way to guarantee that the generosity of the earth would be renewed in the following cycle. Thus, offerings were carefully prepared and placed on outdoor altars, in sacred groves, or near harvested fields. These offerings often consisted of ears of wheat, barley, ripe fruits, and cakes made especially for the occasion. Some accounts mention the custom of burying part of the first harvest in the ground as a symbolic gesture of return, a way of reaffirming respect for the soil that sustained life.

In addition to offerings, celebrations included community feasts, in which freshly baked bread and the first beers made with the season's grains occupied a prominent place. Bread, in particular, held strong symbolism within the festival, representing the essential food and the direct connection between the land and those who feed from it. Some communities shaped bread into symbolic forms, such as spirals and anthropomorphic figures, believing that this practice carried a ritualistic meaning and strengthened the group's prosperity. Beer, an ancestrally linked drink to fertility and celebration, was consumed amid toasts and songs, strengthening community ties.

Games and competitions were also an essential part of the festival. Inspired by Lugh, participants challenged each other in tests of strength, endurance, and skill. Races, fights, stone-throwing competitions, and weapon skill contests were common, reflecting the importance of physical vigor and preparation for times of scarcity. These were not just demonstrations of power, but a way to honor human effort and recognize the need for resilience in the face of the challenges that would come with the colder seasons. In some regions, board games and mental challenges were also held, reinforcing that intelligence was as valuable as strength.

Lughnasadh was not just a festival of material celebration, but also a time for strengthening community ties. It was a time of joy, when people gathered to dance, sing, and tell stories around the fire. The shared narratives often spoke of heroes and ancestors, transmitting wisdom and teachings across generations. Dance and music, in turn, evoked the spirit of the land and the energy of the harvest, creating a vibrant environment of communion.

Beyond the celebration, the festival carried a reflective aspect. With summer reaching its peak and autumn hinting on the horizon, there was an awareness that abundance was fleeting and that the cycle of life was in constant motion. It was a propitious time to evaluate the fruits harvested not only on the land but also in personal life. What had been achieved so far? What challenges had been overcome? What still needed to be improved? These reflections helped individuals prepare for what was to come, encouraging an attitude of gratitude and planning for the future.

Thus, celebrating Lughnasadh was much more than celebrating the harvest; it was an opportunity to honor human effort, recognize the generosity of the land, and strengthen ties with the community and the sacred. The festival taught that prosperity should be shared, that work and dedication are rewarded, and that gratitude is the key to the continuity of abundance. Today, we can connect with this ancient tradition by recognizing the value of what we cultivate - be it on the land, in our relationships, or in our personal projects. By honoring Lughnasadh, we learn to celebrate our achievements, express gratitude, and prepare wisely for the challenges and opportunities of the next cycle.

And so, as the first fruits are harvested and the fields begin to bid farewell to summer, Lughnasadh teaches us that each phase of life brings its rewards and challenges. The harvest is not just the end of a cycle, but the harbinger of a new beginning, where the seeds of the present become the fruits of the future. To honor this moment is to understand that effort and gratitude go hand in hand, sustaining not only the body but also the spirit. May we celebrate our achievements, share our abundance, and move forward with the certainty that each season brings its wisdom.

Chapter 13
Autumn Equinox

The autumn twilight unfolds on the horizon, dyeing the fields and forests with intense colors of red, gold, and amber. The breeze carries the scent of dry leaves and ripe fruits, while the sun gently bows on its journey, announcing the arrival of Mabon, the autumn equinox. This is the sacred moment when light and darkness balance, reflecting the harmony between day and night, between expansion and retreat. The earth, generous in its gift, offers the last fruits of the harvest, and humanity reciprocates with gratitude and reflection. This ancestral cycle, repeated throughout the centuries, teaches that each phase of life has its purpose: if summer was a time of growth and abundance, now comes the time of the final harvest and preparation for the retreat of winter. Mabon invites a close look at what has been cultivated throughout the year, not only in the fields but also in the hearts and individual journeys.

The arrival of the equinox awakens a sense of transition, a call to introspection and gratitude. The ancients knew that the balance between light and shadow was not just an astronomical phenomenon, but a reflection of life in its essence. Nature enters a slower rhythm, the days shorten, and the growth cycle gives way to the need to preserve and store. Just as the fruits of the earth are harvested and stored, this is also a time to gather learnings, acknowledge the efforts made, and reflect on the paths traveled. The duality of the equinox reminds us that life is made of complementary opposites and that for each phase of expansion, there is a moment of pause and renewal. Celebrating Mabon means honoring this cycle, welcoming changes with wisdom, and preparing for the new period that is announced.

The rituals of this period reflect the need for connection with the land and natural cycles. Foods such as apples, grapes, grains, and nuts are symbols of the abundance that Mabon provides and represent gratitude for the generosity of nature. Altars are assembled with elements harvested from the earth, reinforcing the importance of recognizing and giving thanks for what has been received. It is a time for sharing, strengthening community ties, and recognizing the importance of harmony in all aspects of life. The equinox invites a smooth transition between the dynamism of summer and the stillness of winter, remembering that each season brings not only challenges but also opportunities for growth and renewal. Thus, Mabon not only celebrates the final harvest but teaches the wisdom of knowing the right time to let go, to end cycles, and to prepare for what is to come.

Celebrated on September 21st, Mabon marks the second point of balance in the Celtic Wheel of the Year, when day and night meet in perfect harmony. The Sun, on its descending journey, crosses the celestial equator, announcing the arrival of longer nights and shorter days.

This moment of transition is deeply symbolic, representing the threshold between light and darkness, abundance and introspection, movement and pause. For the Celts, this festival held special significance, as it was an occasion to thank the earth for the fruits granted, acknowledge the efforts of the past year, and prepare for the approaching months of retreat.

The celebration of Mabon was directly linked to the agricultural cycle. It was the time of the final harvest, when the last fruits were removed from the fields, and the grains were stored to ensure survival during the winter. This period of transition was seen not only as an act of material preservation but also as a moment of deep reflection. Just as farmers collected the products of the land, people were also invited to harvest the learnings of the year, evaluate their achievements, and say goodbye to what was no longer necessary. The generosity of nature was honored in community rituals, reinforcing the connection between humanity and the natural world.

One of the most striking customs of this festival was the creation of altars decorated with the symbols of the season. Fruits like apples and grapes, vegetables, grains, and flowers were carefully arranged, representing the abundance provided by the earth. Additionally, dry leaves, ears of wheat, pumpkins, and other typical autumn elements adorned homes, reinforcing the aesthetics of the season and gratitude for the fertility cycle that was ending. Autumn colors - red, gold, orange, and brown - predominated, reflecting the warm and welcoming tone of this period.

Thanksgiving rituals also played a central role in Mabon celebrations. Offerings of food and drinks were dedicated to the deities of the harvest and the earth, as a way of expressing gratitude and ensuring the continuity of prosperity in the following cycle. Outdoor feasts were common, where families and communities gathered to share the abundance of the moment, strengthening ties with each other and reaffirming the importance of the spirit of sharing. The act of sharing food symbolized not only the generosity of the season but also the recognition that life is sustained by exchange and mutual support.

In addition to external rites, Mabon was an invitation to introspection and alignment with the inner cycles of life. The balance between light and shadow in the natural world reflected the need to find this same harmony within oneself. It was a propitious time for meditations, for closing cycles, and for releasing what no longer served. Many traditions included writing rituals, where people wrote down everything they wanted to leave behind and burned the paper as a symbolic act of transformation and renewal. Conscious gratitude was also practiced, listing all the blessings received throughout the year, reinforcing the connection with positivity and abundance.

The connection with ancestors and ancestral wisdom was another important aspect of this celebration. The Celts believed that this was a period when the veil between worlds became thinner, allowing deeper contact with those who came before. Thus, paying homage to ancestors and seeking inspiration from their teachings was part of the Mabon rituals. Candles were lit in their memories, stories were told in family gatherings, and herbs were burned for purification and protection.

Nature offered countless symbolic elements that were incorporated into celebrations. Apples, for example, represented knowledge and immortality, being used in spells and offerings. Wine, made from harvested grapes, symbolized transformation and the passage of time. Nuts and seeds reinforced the idea that everything harvested now will serve the future, both literally and spiritually. Small rituals with these elements were performed, such as burying an apple as an offering to the earth or keeping a special seed to plant the following spring, symbolizing the continuity of life.

Mabon was also a time of balance between the masculine and feminine aspects of nature. As summer, associated with solar strength and active energy, came to an end, winter, linked to introspection and retreat, began to approach. This balance was reflected in the duality present within each individual, remembering that there is a time to act and a time to rest, a time to expand and a time to internalize. Recognizing and accepting these natural rhythms allowed for deeper alignment with the wisdom of the earth.

In short, Mabon was not just a harvest festival but a ritual of balance, gratitude, and renewal. Celebrating this moment meant honoring the cycle of life, recognizing the importance of letting go of what has served its purpose, and preparing for what is to come. The energy of this equinox invites us to look inward, to value our achievements, and to set intentions for the new cycle that begins. By connecting with this ancestral tradition, we can not only give thanks for the abundance received but also learn to flow with the natural rhythms of existence, welcoming each season with wisdom and gratitude.

And so, as the leaves dance in the wind and the days slowly give way to night, Mabon reminds us of the beauty of balance and the need to embrace change with serenity. The harvest ends a cycle, but it also plants the seeds of what is yet to come, teaching that each farewell carries within it the promise of a new beginning. May we carry in our hearts gratitude for what has been achieved, the wisdom to let go of what has served its purpose, and the clarity to walk with confidence towards the next cycle of the journey.

Chapter 14
Sacred Places

The Celtic landscape was much more than a natural setting; it was a reflection of the sacred, a living territory where earth, water, sky, and stones intertwined in an eternal dance of energy and spiritual significance. Each place carried a unique presence, imbued with myths, stories, and invisible forces that guided the ancient people in their connection with the divine. Specific locations, marked by their imposing beauty or extraordinary natural phenomena, were revered as portals to the Otherworld, spaces where the veil between dimensions became thinner and communication with gods, spirits, and ancestors was more accessible. For the Celts, each element of nature possessed its own spirit, and recognizing this sacredness was fundamental to living in harmony with the cosmic flow. These places were not just points of worship, but centers of wisdom, healing, and protection, resonating with the energy of the universe and offering guidance to those seeking answers on their spiritual journeys.

In the ancestral forests, the Celts saw natural temples where trees, especially oak, ash, and yew, were guardians of ancient secrets. Considered living beings endowed with soul and consciousness, these green giants formed mystical corridors leading to the unknown. Hidden clearings under the canopy of trees served as natural altars, where druids performed rituals, healing ceremonies, and seasonal festivals. Similarly, sacred waters, such as rivers, springs, and wells, were seen as direct channels for purification and spiritual renewal. It was believed that their currents carried messages from the gods and that immersing oneself in their waters or offering them tributes could bring healing and blessings. Each spring or river possessed a unique energy, and many were dedicated to female deities, representations of fertility and nourishment that the earth bestowed upon its children.

The mountains, with their imposing heights and silhouettes challenging the sky, were seen as places of great power, where contact with the divine became more intense. Many peaks were considered dwellings of gods or protective spirits, being pilgrimage destinations for those seeking enlightenment and strength. Similarly, sacred stones, whether in the form of solitary menhirs, stone circles, or imposing natural formations, carried the weight of time and history, serving as anchors of cosmic energy. These silent monuments were used for spiritual alignment, healing, and communication with the Otherworld. Each of these places contained its own mystery, a distinct vibration that resonated with the journey of those who visited them. Honoring these spaces was, for the Celts, to recognize the sacredness of existence and reaffirm the eternal bond between humanity, nature, and divinity.

Celtic forests, vast and dense, were more than mere agglomerations of trees; they were living portals to the Otherworld, the domain of gods and ancestors. Each imposing trunk and rustling leaf told a story, and the Celts believed that certain trees possessed a sacred essence, an ancestral soul that harbored deep secrets and a wisdom lost in time. Oak, yew, and ash were particularly revered, as it was believed that their roots plunged into the depths of the earth, connecting the world of the living to that of spirits. Their branches rose towards the sky, forming an invisible bridge between the earthly and the divine.

The groves of these trees were considered to be inhabited by nature spirits, ethereal beings who protected the secrets of the Otherworld and guided those who were ready to understand the mysteries of existence. It was common for druids, guardians of Celtic tradition and knowledge, to perform their rituals in hidden clearings, where sunlight filtered through the leaves in golden beams, creating a magical environment charged with spiritual energy. In these ceremonies, they chanted sacred songs, made offerings to the deities, and invoked the forces of the forest for protection, healing, and wisdom. These clearings were true natural temples, places where the connection between man and nature became more tangible and where the mysteries of the universe could be unveiled by those who knew how to listen.

Like forests, the waters of rivers and springs were seen as direct manifestations of sacredness, sources of life and purification. Each drop that sprang from the earth or flowed in streams was considered to carry healing and magical powers. The Celts believed that the waters were inhabited by female deities and water spirits who bestowed blessings on those who respected their dwelling. In many places, sacred wells were dedicated to specific goddesses of fertility and healing, and pilgrims traveled great distances to bathe in their waters or cast offerings – coins, jewels, or small personal objects – as a way of asking for protection and spiritual guidance.

Purification rituals performed on the banks of rivers were common practices, involving ceremonial baths and the immersion of the faithful in search of renewal and healing. Water was an essential element for balancing body and spirit, cleansing negative energies and allowing the vital flow to realign with cosmic harmony. In some places, springs were considered natural oracles, and priests interpreted the ripples and reflections of the water to predict the future or receive messages from the gods.

Rising above the Celtic lands, the mountains dominated the landscape with their grandeur and mystery. For these people, these colossal rock formations were not just geographical features, but pillars that sustained the connection between the human world and the divine. Their summits, often shrouded in mist, were seen as access points to the Otherworld, places where the barrier between realms became more fragile and communication with the gods was clearer. Many mountains were associated with specific deities or legendary heroes who, according to stories, had climbed their peaks in search of wisdom or spiritual challenges.

Pilgrimages to sacred mountains were rites of passage, journeys of self-discovery and transformation. Climbing to the top was considered an act of courage and faith, as it required physical effort and spiritual endurance. Those who undertook this journey often returned with a renewed vision of themselves and their purpose, as if the altitude granted them a broader perspective of destiny and the forces that governed the universe. Some of these mountains were also settings for druidic rites and seasonal festivals, where people gathered to celebrate the passage of time and the renewal of natural energies.

In addition to sacred trees, life-giving waters, and imposing mountains, there were stones – silent witnesses of time and guardians of ancestral power. The Celts believed that certain monoliths and rock formations possessed concentrated energies, being portals to the Otherworld or points of connection with spiritual forces. Solitary menhirs, erected by unknown hands millennia ago, were considered landmarks of power, capable of channeling energies and protecting those who lived around them. Stone circles, like the famous Stonehenge, were open-air temples used for astronomical alignments, sacred rituals, and communion with the gods.

Rituals performed in these places involved dances, chants, and deep meditations. Each stone, meticulously arranged, resonated with the energy of the earth and the cosmos, and the position of the stars was often taken into account to determine the ideal time for ceremonies. It was common for druids to use stones to channel healing, laying their hands on their surfaces or placing the sick around them to absorb the emanating energy.

Each of these sacred places had its own story, a myth that explained its origin and meaning. Some were dedicated to specific deities, receiving offerings and prayers constantly, while others were revered simply for their imposing beauty and mystical aura. The act of pilgrimage to these points was seen as a way to align oneself with the flow of nature, strengthening the bond between men and gods.

Ultimately, Celtic sacred places were much more than places of worship; they were living expressions of the spirituality of these people and their relationship with the universe. They represented the belief in the sacredness present in all elements of nature, in the pulsating energy that connected every living being to the great web of existence. For the Celts, honoring these places was a way to reaffirm their belonging to a sacred and harmonious cosmos. Today, as we learn about and contemplate these places, we can feel remnants of this ancestral connection and, perhaps, find inspiration for our own spiritual journey.

The echoes of sacred places still resonate in the present, as living memories of the deep connection between the ancient Celts and the land that welcomed them. Their forests, rivers, mountains, and stones continue to hold secrets for those who know how to listen, reminding us that the sacred is not only in these distant places, but in every leaf, in every breath of wind, and in every heartbeat. By recognizing the sacredness that permeates the natural world, we rediscover a lost bond and rediscover the wisdom that invites us to live in harmony with the cycles of existence, just as those who came before us did.

Chapter 15
Sacred Trees

Trees occupied a central place in Celtic spirituality, being revered as sacred entities, sources of knowledge, and a link between the visible and invisible worlds. Far from being just natural elements, they were recognized as beings endowed with consciousness, possessing a living essence that transcended time and space. For the Celts, each tree carried a unique energy, a wisdom of its own that influenced both the balance of nature and human destinies. Entire groves were consecrated to the worship of these trees, where rituals, ceremonies, and magical practices unfolded under the protection of their ancestral canopies. The presence of trees in Celtic life was not limited to the physical plane, but extended to the mystical sphere, connecting men to the deities and the knowledge of their ancestors. The relationship between the Celts and trees was not only one of veneration, but also of learning, as they found in them lessons of resilience, renewal, and harmony with the universe.

The symbolic strength of sacred trees was reflected in their ritual uses, in their influence on myths, and in their association with deities and cosmic forces. Among all, the oak stood out as the most powerful, representing the connection with the divine and the wisdom of the druids, who performed ceremonies under its majestic presence. The yew, with its regenerative capacity, symbolized the continuity of life beyond death, being a portal to the Otherworld. The ash, with its deep roots and imposing trunk, was seen as the World Tree, sustaining the connection between the three planes of existence. Other species, such as hazel, apple, and willow, also played essential roles, either as sources of inspiration and knowledge, or as instruments of magic and protection. In each leaf, fruit, and trunk, the Celts saw hidden messages and invisible forces, understanding that nature not only offered shelter and sustenance, but also answers to the mysteries of existence.

Celtic spirituality manifested itself in the way these trees were integrated into everyday life, serving as guides on life's journey. Amulets made from their branches, infusions prepared with their leaves, and rituals performed under their shade demonstrated the deep belief that trees were guardians of the cosmic order and possessors of balance between the elements. Respecting and understanding sacred trees meant honoring natural cycles and living in tune with the Earth and its powers. This relationship transcended time, echoing even today in how connection with nature can bring valuable lessons about strength, renewal, and harmony. By immersing ourselves in the universe of Celtic sacred trees, we not only understand their culture and spirituality, but also reclaim the importance of a deep and respectful relationship with the natural world.

The oak, imposing in its grandeur and possessor of a longevity that spans eras, reigned supreme among the sacred trees. Considered the king of the forest, it symbolized unwavering strength, resistance to time, and profound wisdom. It was not just a tree; it was a pillar of Celtic spirituality, a bridge between the earthly world and the divine. The druids, guardians of ancestral knowledge, chose oak groves for their ceremonies and rituals, believing that there, under their sturdy canopies, they could access the wisdom of the gods and receive mystical revelations. Each oak was seen as a sacred dwelling, where powerful deities resided, granting protection and guidance to those who paid them reverence. Its acorns, small jewels of the forest, were not only a source of food, but carried magical properties within them, being used in healing rituals, protective amulets, and even as oracles to predict destiny. To be under an oak was not just to find shade and shelter; it was to feel the living presence of Celtic spirituality pulsating in the ancient wood, in the leaves dancing in the wind, and in the roots that plunged into the depths of the earth, connecting to the heart of the world.

The yew, with its evergreen foliage and its mysterious ability to regenerate, held an even deeper meaning within Celtic symbolism. For these people, it represented not only longevity, but the infinite cycle of life, death, and rebirth. Associated with the Otherworld, the domain of spirits and ancestors, it was common to find yews planted near cemeteries and burial sites, as it was believed that these trees served as portals between the living and those who had departed. The yew was the very essence of immortality, demonstrating that death was not an end, but merely a transition to a new form of existence. Its leaves and fruits, although poisonous, were used with extreme respect in rites of passage and spiritual protection. Under its shade, the Celts meditated on the mysteries of existence, seeking to understand the secrets of eternity and the path their souls would follow after earthly life. On nights of rituals, it was common for druids to use yew branches to trace sacred symbols on the ground, invoking the protection of ancestral spirits and asking for guidance for the challenges of the present and future.

The ash, with its firm, resistant, and yet flexible wood, was a symbol of strength and adaptation, essential qualities for those who wished to tread a wise and balanced path. For the Celts, it was not just a tree, but the very Tree of Life, the one that sustained the three planes of existence: heaven, earth, and the underworld. Its roots plunged deep, its trunk rose firmly, and its branches touched the heavens, forming a connection that transcended the limits of the physical world. Ash was used in the making of weapons and tools, as it was believed that its wood carried the essence of protection and courage. In addition, ash leaves and seeds were often used in the preparation of healing potions and protective amulets, as it was believed that this tree had the power to ward off disease and bad influences. In mythological narratives, the ash often appeared as a tree of divine origin, a cosmic axis that maintained the order of the universe and guided those who sought to understand the mysteries of existence.

The hazel, in turn, was the tree of wisdom, inspiration, and connection to the secrets of the universe. Its presence was considered an omen of deep knowledge and spiritual revelations. It was believed that whoever ate its hazelnuts immediately acquired an expanded vision of the world, awakening gifts of prophecy and divination. Celtic bards and poets revered the hazel, seeking in it inspiration for their compositions and stories. Many magic wands were made of its wood, as it carried the essence of intuition and discernment. In rituals, its leaves and fruits were used in divination practices, aiding those who sought answers about the future or needed to make important decisions. In sacred groves, streams flowed alongside ancient hazels, and legends told that their roots touched sources of wisdom hidden in the depths of the earth. Sitting in the shade of a hazel, in meditation, was a common practice among those who wished to access mental clarity and better understand the designs of the gods.

The apple tree, with its delicate beauty and irresistible fruits, played an essential role in Celtic myths and rituals. Associated with love, fertility, and immortality, it was seen as the goddess's tree, a symbol of the union between the human and divine worlds. The Celts believed that apples had magical properties and that those who ate them could experience prophetic visions or even achieve eternal youth. The apple tree was present in the tales of heroes and legends about enchanted lands, where its golden fruits were offered as proof of divine blessing. Its flowering branches were used in love rituals, and its petals were scattered on altars to attract harmony and prosperity. In marriage ceremonies, it was common to present the bride and groom with apples, wishing them a long and fruitful union. More than a symbol of sweetness and abundance, the apple tree represented the very cycle of life, with its flowers that bloomed in spring, its fruits that ripened in autumn, and its leaves that fell in winter, only to be reborn with renewed vigor the following year.

The willow, with its flexible branches and its intimate connection with water, was seen as the tree of intuition, emotion, and healing. Always growing on the banks of rivers and lakes, it seemed to whisper secrets to the wind and reflect the feelings of those who approached its roots. Associated with the goddess and lunar powers, the willow was a tree of transformation and magic. Its leaves and bark were used in the preparation of healing infusions, while its branches were used in the making of baskets and sacred instruments. During purification rituals, it was common for the Celts to dip willow branches in water and sprinkle the liquid on those seeking renewal and spiritual balance. The willow was also a guide for dreams and visions; many traditions claimed that sleeping under its canopy could bring revelations from the Otherworld, messages from the gods, or visits from ancestors. With its melancholic yet deeply welcoming appearance, this tree reminded the Celts that emotions were as fluid as rivers and that, like water, the soul needed to flow freely to find its true path.

Each of these sacred trees represented an essential aspect of Celtic spirituality, manifesting the teachings of nature and the connection with cosmic forces. For the Celts, honoring trees was not just an act of veneration, but a recognition that life itself was a continuous cycle of learning, renewal, and harmony. Through the wisdom of these trees, they understood the importance of living in balance with the earth and the elements, respecting the rhythms of nature and always seeking communion with the sacred.

Thus, as we contemplate the sacred trees of the Celts, we realize that they were not only symbols of power and spirituality, but also living witnesses to the deep connection between humans and nature. Each trunk that resists time, each leaf that dances in the wind, and each root that intertwines with the earth reminds us that wisdom is present in each cycle, in each transformation. Honoring these trees is more than revering the past; it is rescuing the essence of an ancestral knowledge that teaches us about strength, renewal, and balance. For, as the Celts knew, by listening to the silent voice of the trees, we learn, at last, the language of life itself.

Chapter 16
Sacred Animals

In the Celtic worldview, animals were much more than mere creatures of nature; they were living symbols of spiritual forces, manifestations of the sacred, and bearers of messages from the Otherworld. Each animal held a deep meaning and was associated with specific qualities that reflected the essence of life and the universe. It was believed that these creatures possessed ancestral knowledge and that their presence could influence the destiny of men, offering protection, guidance, and power. The Celts closely observed the habits and behaviors of animals, interpreting their signs as omens and valuable lessons for the earthly journey. The relationship between humans and animals was permeated by respect, admiration, and reverence, as it was understood that through these creatures, the gods and spirits of nature communicated directly with mortals.

The strong connection between the Celts and the sacred animals was reflected in their spiritual beliefs and rituals. Many warriors adopted the strength and courage of totemic animals as inspiration for their battles, while the druids, wise men and priests, used animal symbolism to decipher spiritual messages and understand the mysteries of the universe. The bear, for example, represented power and leadership, guiding those who sought courage and resilience. The raven, with its intelligence and mysticism, was a messenger between the worlds, carrying with it the hidden knowledge of the gods. The boar symbolized determination and bravery, being an example of persistence in the face of life's challenges. The salmon, with its tireless journey against the current, was an archetype of the search for wisdom and the return to spiritual origins. Each creature, with its unique strength, was part of a sacred web that interconnected all beings and elements of existence.

Celtic spirituality not only recognized the importance of animals but also celebrated them as allies in the human journey toward understanding the divine. The horse, with its majesty and loyalty, represented freedom and nobility, often being associated with travel between the physical and spiritual worlds. The deer, in turn, symbolized renewal and connection with the natural cycles of life. These creatures, in addition to inspiring the Celts in their relationship with the natural world, reinforced the belief that harmony between humans, animals, and cosmic forces was essential for the fullness of existence. By understanding the symbolism of sacred animals, we not only delve into Celtic thought but also rescue a worldview where nature and the sacred are intertwined, teaching us to live with more respect, balance, and harmony with the universe.

The bear, imposing and majestic, occupied a central place in Celtic symbolism, being considered the king of animals. Its brute strength and dominant presence made it a symbol of unquestionable power, but its essence went beyond mere physical brutality. The Celts saw in the bear the representation of courage and leadership, indispensable qualities for those who needed to face battles, both in the physical and spiritual fields. It was believed that this totemic animal was a guardian of the forests and communities, protecting those who invoked its strength. Furthermore, its ability to hibernate and then emerge renewed made the bear an archetype of transformation and rebirth, a mirror of the cyclical nature of life itself. For Celtic warriors, connecting spiritually with the bear meant absorbing its determination and indomitable spirit, becoming invincible in the face of challenges. In many rituals, the druids evoked the energy of this great animal to strengthen the warriors and ensure the protection of the territories, believing that the bear carried with it a direct link to the spiritual world.

The boar, in turn, was one of the most respected symbols of bravery and determination in the Celtic universe. Wild and ferocious, this animal did not back down from danger, facing any adversity with unwavering courage. Its ability to survive in hostile environments and fight fiercely to protect its territory was seen as a supreme example of willpower and resilience. The Celts deeply admired this indomitable nature and, therefore, warriors often wore boar skins or tusks as amulets, believing that such objects would confer courage and resistance in combat. In addition, the boar had a strong connection to the earth and the mysteries of the forest, being associated with fertility and abundance. Feasts and rituals dedicated to this animal were common, and its meat was considered sacred food in ceremonial banquets. Among the legendary stories, the boar often appeared as a challenging creature that tested the courage of heroes, symbolizing the need to face one's own fears to achieve spiritual growth.

The raven, with its sharp intelligence and enigmatic flight, occupied a unique position in Celtic mythology. This black bird was seen as a messenger between the worlds, carrying with it secrets from the Otherworld and revelations from the gods. Its croaking was interpreted as a warning, and its unexpected appearance was considered an omen that could indicate both protection and destruction. The Celts believed that the raven guided the souls of the dead on their afterlife journey, serving as a guardian of spiritual mysteries. This dual aspect of the bird—between life and death, between wisdom and omen—made it a powerful symbol of transformation and renewal. Among the druids, the raven was revered as a bearer of hidden knowledge, and many practitioners of magic and divination sought to interpret its behavior to unravel messages from beyond. In addition, the raven was strongly associated with the goddesses of war, such as Morrigan, who assumed its form on the battlefields to predict the fate of the combatants. This link between the raven and war reflected the Celtic belief that knowledge and strategy were as essential to victory as brute strength.

The salmon, in contrast, was a symbol of wisdom and persistence. This fish, known for its arduous journey against the current to reach its spawning ground, inspired the Celts to never give up on their goals, even when the path was fraught with obstacles. The story of the Salmon of Wisdom, present in Irish mythology, illustrates this belief well: it was said that an ancient salmon, upon feeding on hazelnuts fallen from a sacred tree, acquired all the knowledge of the world. Whoever ate it, in turn, would inherit its wisdom. Thus, the salmon became an archetype of the search for knowledge, the connection with ancestry, and the ability to return to spiritual origins. The druids valued its symbolism and saw in the life cycle of this fish a representation of the soul's journey, which goes through countless challenges to achieve enlightenment. In addition, the salmon was also related to intuition and memory, being considered a guide for those who sought answers within themselves.

The horse, with its beauty and majesty, was one of the animals most revered by the Celts, representing freedom, strength, and nobility. Since ancient times, horses were essential for the survival of these people, being used both in battles and in transportation and agriculture. However, their importance transcended the practical aspect, as the Celts believed that these animals possessed mystical powers and were able to travel between worlds. Many Celtic deities were associated with horses, such as Epona, the patron goddess of horses, fertility, and travel. She was worshiped not only by the Celts but also by the Romans, who recognized her importance and incorporated her into their pantheon. In addition, the horse was considered a conductor of souls, guiding the spirits of the dead to the Otherworld. The presence of this animal in funerary rituals and its representation in sculptures and archaeological artifacts reinforce its connection to Celtic spirituality. In many traditions, riding a horse was seen as a symbolic act of dominion over the forces of nature and the connection between man and the divine.

Finally, the deer, with its grace and majesty, symbolized the life force of nature and the renewal of life. The Celts saw in this animal a representation of fertility and abundance, associating its antlers with the Tree of Life, which connected heaven and earth. The deer was often portrayed as a messenger of the gods, a guide that led human beings to spiritual enlightenment. Its presence in sacred forests was considered a sign of blessing, and many believed that following it could lead to profound revelations. Some legends describe warriors and hunters who, while chasing a mystical deer, ended up being led to magical realms, where they learned valuable lessons about themselves and the world. For the druids, the deer represented harmony with nature and the need to respect the cycles of life. Its antlers, which fell off and grew back, symbolized constant renewal and the ability to start over. Thus, this sacred animal inspired the Celts to seek a balanced existence aligned with natural forces.

Celtic sacred animals were not just symbolic figures but living representations of the cosmic forces that governed the universe. Each creature carried with it a valuable lesson, a unique power, and a deep connection to the sacred. Through observation and respect for these beings, the Celts found ways to understand themselves and the world around them, reaffirming their belief in the interconnection between all living beings and the presence of the divine in every aspect of existence.

By recognizing animals as manifestations of the sacred, the Celts reinforced the idea that nature was an extension of the divine, a living reflection of the mysteries of the universe. Each creature, with its unique strengths and symbolism, served as a link between men and the gods, guiding mortals through signs and hidden teachings. This vision not only strengthened their spirituality but also shaped their relationship with the natural world, based on respect and harmony. Thus, sacred animals were not just mythical figures or power totems, but spiritual companions that helped the Celts to tread their journey on Earth, always in search of balance, wisdom, and connection with the eternal.

Chapter 17
Celtic Magic

Celtic magic was a living force that flowed through all elements of existence, intertwining the visible and the invisible, the natural and the spiritual, the past and the future. More than a set of spells or occult practices, this magical tradition was a reflection of the deep connection of the Celts with nature and the cycles of life. Everything in the world possessed a spirit and a sacred energy, from the breath of the wind to the sap that flowed in the ancestral trees. The Celts understood that magic was not a tool to manipulate reality, but rather a means of interacting with cosmic forces in balance and respect. The harmony between the elements and the understanding of the signs of nature were fundamental to accessing this hidden knowledge and channeling its power for healing, protection, and transformation.

The druids, wise men and guardians of mystical knowledge, were the main mediators of Celtic magic. They were the ones who mastered the secrets of herbs, stones, and lunar cycles, understanding the flows of energy that connected the different realms of existence. Celtic magical practice was based on the observation of nature and the belief that each element had a guardian spirit, capable of offering guidance and power to those who knew how to listen to it. Sacred groves, stone circles, and crystal-clear springs were considered portals to other dimensions, where the gods and ancestors could be contacted. In ceremonies held under the moonlight or during seasonal festivals, the Celts invoked these energies to strengthen the community and align themselves with the natural rhythms of the universe.

In addition to rituals and enchantments, Celtic magic also manifested itself in the creation of amulets and talismans, objects charged with meaning and power. Runes were engraved on stones, symbols were intertwined in fabrics, and specific herbs were gathered for protection or spiritual strengthening. The Celts understood that everything around them could be a channel for magic, from the flight of a bird to the arrangement of fallen leaves on the ground. Living in tune with this vision meant respecting the sacredness of the world and understanding that true magic lay in connection with the earth, the sky, and the spirits that inhabited both realms. Today, as we study Celtic magic, we can rescue this ancestral understanding and apply it as a path of balance, wisdom, and harmony with the invisible forces that shape our reality.

The Celts believed that the universe was permeated by a vital energy, an invisible and pulsating force that animated all things, connecting them in a subtle and inseparable web. This energy, called awen, flowed incessantly through nature, human beings, and the gods, forming a link between the visible and the invisible, the earthly and the divine. For the Celts, understanding and manipulating this force meant aligning oneself with the rhythms of the cosmos, respecting the cycles of life, and using magic as a means of interaction, never domination. Celtic magic, therefore, was not seen as a mere instrument of power, but as a practice of communion with universal energies, allowing them to be directed towards healing, protection, prosperity, and transformation.

Druids, the sages and masters of this tradition, were the guardians of ancestral knowledge and the main mediators of Celtic magic. Deeply knowledgeable about herbs, stones, stars, and the elements, they possessed the ability to interpret the signs of nature and used this wisdom to perform rituals, enchantments, and spells. Druidic practice was not based on the imposition of wills, but on careful observation of natural cycles, reading omens, and respectful interaction with the spirits of the earth. These priests understood that everything in the world had a sacred essence and that every being, be it a towering tree, a mighty river, or a silent mountain, carried within it a fragment of the divine.

Celtic magic manifested itself in various aspects of everyday life, transcending grand rituals to integrate into the daily lives of its people. Trees were seen as pillars between worlds, linking heaven, earth, and the underworld, and were revered with offerings and prayers. Rivers and springs, considered portals to the realm of spirits, were places of purification and spiritual connection. Animals, in turn, were seen as messengers of the gods, bringing omens and teachings to those who knew how to interpret their signs. This deep connection with nature caused the Celts to see magic in everything around them—in the flight of a bird, in the pattern of the clouds, in the murmur of the wind through the leaves.

Among the most common magical practices was the use of amulets, talismans, and jewelry, objects imbued with symbolism and power. These items were made with carefully chosen materials, such as specific stones, consecrated metals, and herbs with magical properties. The Celts believed that such objects could channel the energies of the universe, serving as bridges between the material and spiritual worlds. A warrior, for example, could carry an amulet carved with runes of protection before a battle, while a pregnant woman could wear a talisman blessed by the druids to ensure a safe and harmonious birth.

Rituals and ceremonies were fundamental pillars of Celtic magic, being performed in sacred places such as ancestral groves, imposing mountains, and stone circles aligned with the stars. These gatherings had various purposes: to celebrate the cycles of nature, to honor the gods, to ask for blessings for the harvests, or to strengthen community ties. During the ceremonies, the druids chanted songs and recited incantations, while ritual dances and offerings were performed to invoke cosmic energies. The sacred fire, a symbol of transformation and rebirth, often burned in the center of the rituals, serving as a point of convergence between the worlds.

Celtic magic, however, was not limited to external manifestations. It was, above all, a path of inner transformation, a means of spiritual growth and evolution. The Celts believed that true magic was not only in spells or rituals but in the way each individual connected with life, with their own gifts, and with the natural flow of the universe. Thus, a simple act of contemplation of nature, a moment of silence before the sea, or a solitary walk through the forest could be as magical as a grand ritual conducted by druids. Magic was everywhere—you just had to know how to see it.

This worldview, centered on interconnection and respect for invisible forces, caused the Celts to always seek harmony with the sacred. They understood that magic was an expression of the very essence of life, an eternal dance between the visible and the hidden, between what is known and what is yet to be discovered. Today, as we study this ancestral tradition, we can rescue its wisdom and apply it in our own journeys, whether through meditation, contemplation of nature, or the creation of personal rituals that connect us with the vital energy that permeates all things. In this way, Celtic magic continues to live, flowing like an eternal river through time and space, uniting those who seek to understand and honor the mysteries of the universe.

Celtic magic, rooted in the harmony between man and nature, transcends time and continues to inspire those who seek a deeper connection with the world around them. Whether in the ancestral rituals of the druids or in the simple contemplation of natural cycles, this tradition teaches us that true power does not lie in domination, but in communion with the subtle forces of the universe. By recognizing the sacredness present in every being, in every breath of wind and in every drop of water, we rediscover magic not as something distant or unattainable, but as an essential part of existence itself.

Chapter 18
Magical Herbology

Celtic magical herbology was a sacred practice that united botanical knowledge, spirituality, and magic, recognizing in plants not only their medicinal properties but also their energies and influence on human destiny. For the Celts, each herb had its own spirit and was connected to the forces of nature, being able to channel cosmic energies and act as a bridge between the physical and spiritual world. The study of herbs was not merely practical knowledge, but a path of deep learning, requiring respect for the cycles of the earth and the living essence of plants. Each leaf, flower, or root was considered a receptacle of power, capable of aiding in healing, protection, purification, and transformation of reality.

The Druids, guardians of Celtic tradition, were the great masters of magical herbology, passing their knowledge down through generations. They knew the exact moment to harvest each herb, respecting astral alignments and moon cycles to enhance its strength. Harvesting was never done impulsively or carelessly; there were specific rituals that ensured that the spirit of the plant would grant its benefits harmoniously. Some herbs were associated with deities, others served as talismans against evil forces, and many were used in potions and incenses to strengthen spiritual connection. Celtic belief held that plants not only cured illnesses of the body but also purified the mind, balanced emotions, and expanded spiritual perception.

The use of herbs in Celtic magic was vast and varied, ranging from simple infusions to complex rituals of protection and divination. Mistletoe, for example, was revered as a plant of immortality and divine power, while verbena was considered an herb of purification and luck. Artemisia and belladonna were used to enhance intuition and facilitate contact with the Otherworld, while yarrow was a symbol of healing and courage. Even common plants, like nettle, had special significance, being used to ward off negative energies and strengthen the body and spirit. Celtic magical herbology teaches us that nature offers abundant resources for balance and well-being, as long as we know how to respect it and attune ourselves to its ancestral wisdom.

The Druids, guardians of ancestral wisdom, dedicated their lives to the study of magical herbology, a knowledge that transcended the merely medicinal use of plants and delved into their spiritual and energetic aspects. Learning this art was not a quick or simple process; on the contrary, it required years of observation, experience, and attunement to the rhythms of nature. They understood that each herb possessed its own spirit and unique magical essence, and that its harvesting and use should be carried out with respect and reverence. Thus, before harvesting any plant, they performed rituals of thanksgiving to the earth and the spirit of the herb, ensuring that its use was harmonious and effective.

The timing of the harvest was crucial to potentiate the effects of the herbs, and the Druids followed lunar calendars and seasonal cycles to determine the exact moment when a plant was at its energetic peak. Some herbs were harvested at sunrise, when dew still covered their leaves and carried the purity of dawn; others, under the light of the full moon, when their connection to the spiritual world was intensified. In addition, specific tools were used in the harvest, such as golden sickles to cut mistletoe without it touching the ground, a symbolic gesture that preserved its purity and power.

Once harvested, the herbs were prepared with carefully studied methods to preserve and amplify their properties. Air drying, maceration in oils, or infusions in pure water were some of the techniques used, always accompanied by prayers and enchantments that directed their energies towards the desired purpose. The preparation of herbs was not a mechanical act, but a ritualistic process in which the Druid's intention was fundamental to activate their magical properties. It was believed that the way an herb was handled directly influenced its effectiveness, and so the Druids taught their apprentices the importance of concentration and respect throughout the process.

These herbs were used in various practices, from curing illnesses and protecting against evil forces to enhancing intuition and strengthening the spirit. Potions were prepared with precise combinations of plants, creating elixirs that balanced body and mind. Ointments were formulated to relieve pain, accelerate wound healing, and strengthen the body against disease. Incense was burned in ceremonies for purification and spiritual elevation, while amulets made with dried herbs were carried as talismans for protection and good luck.

Among the most revered plants in Celtic magical herbology, mistletoe stood out as a symbol of immortality and protection. Considered sacred, it was harvested with extreme care and used in healing and fertility rituals. Its presence in homes warded off negative influences and brought blessings to the inhabitants. Verbena, known as the "sacred herb", was widely used in rituals of purification, love, and prosperity. Its aroma was considered capable of cleansing environments of heavy energies and attracting harmony.

Mugwort, consecrated to the goddess Artemis, was valued for its ability to provide spiritual protection and enhance perception. Its use in pillows helped ward off nightmares and facilitate prophetic dreams. Belladonna, despite its danger, was used with extreme caution in divination practices and communication with the Otherworld. Its hallucinogenic effects were feared and respected, and only the most experienced dared to use it.

Yarrow, also called the "soldier's herb", was a powerful ally in healing wounds, stopping bleeding, and preventing infections. In addition to its physical properties, it was considered a symbol of courage and protection, being used by warriors before battles. Nettle, despite its reputation as an aggressive plant, had a vast medicinal and magical use. It strengthened the body, purified the blood, and warded off negative influences, being used in cleansing baths and protection rituals.

The Celtic view of magical herbology did not separate the physical from the spiritual. For them, each plant carried a unique vibration that could act on different levels of the human being, promoting not only the healing of the body but also emotional balance and the expansion of consciousness. Respect for nature and attunement to its rhythms were fundamental for the power of herbs to be fully accessed.

Those who wished to learn this art needed not only to study the properties of plants, but also to develop a deep connection with the earth and its cycles. Careful observation of the seasons, understanding lunar influences, and respect for the spirits of nature were essential requirements for a true Celtic herbalist. The practice of magical herbology was not just a science, but a spiritual path, a way of honoring life and the sacred that dwells in every leaf, root, and flower.

Thus, the ancestral wisdom of the Druids continues to echo through the centuries, inspiring those who seek to reconnect with the magic of herbs and the natural balance of the universe. Celtic magical herbology teaches us that the true power of plants goes beyond their healing or mystical properties; it lies in the relationship of respect and attunement that we cultivate with nature. For the Celts, each herb was a gift from the gods, a fragment of universal energy accessible to those who knew how to listen to it and use it wisely. This ancestral knowledge continues to live, reminding us that magic is in the earth beneath our feet, in the leaves that dance in the wind, and in the invisible harmony that connects all beings. By rescuing this vision, we not only honor the legacy of the Druids, but also bring ourselves closer to the sacred balance that governs life.

Chapter 19
Crystals and Stones

The Celts saw the mineral world as a sacred manifestation of the earth's energy, full of strength and ancestral wisdom. For them, crystals and stones were not just inert elements, but bearers of power, capable of influencing human destinies, strengthening the connection with the divine, and serving as tools for healing and protection. It was believed that each stone had a unique vibration, resonating with different aspects of existence and interacting with the energy of living beings. Thus, the use of crystals was part of daily life, spiritual rituals, and the construction of sacred monuments, uniting the Celtic people with the essence of nature and the balance of the cosmos.

Druids, priests, and sages of Celtic culture mastered the knowledge of the energetic properties of crystals and knew how to use them to strengthen the spirit and align natural forces. Stones were chosen based on their characteristics, colors, and astrological associations, being used both in the making of amulets and in the creation of sacred spaces, such as stone circles. Some crystals were used to attract prosperity and courage, while others were valued for their ability to protect against negative influences or facilitate communication with the Otherworld. It was believed that the energy of stones could be amplified through rituals and intentions, making them powerful allies for those seeking spiritual growth, emotional balance, and connection with the divine.

In addition to precious and semi-precious crystals, the Celts also recognized the power of natural stones found in fields, rivers, and mountains. Menhirs and dolmens were erected in strategic locations, channeling telluric energies and serving as meeting points between the earthly and spiritual worlds. Stone circles, like the famous Stonehenge, reflected this deep understanding of the influence of minerals on the earth's energy and cosmic cycles. The Celtic tradition teaches us that crystals and stones are not mere ornaments, but living instruments of strength and wisdom, capable of transforming our perception of the world and guiding us in our search for harmony and the sacred.

Druids held a deep knowledge of crystals and their energetic properties. For them, these stones were more than mere adornments; they were bearers of primordial forces, capable of influencing the energy of living beings and serving as bridges between the material and spiritual worlds. Each crystal was carefully chosen, taking into account its astrological correspondences, its relationship with the elements, and its affinity with certain magical intentions. This selection process was not random, but rather a ritual in itself, carried out with deep respect and purpose, aiming to maximize the effects of the stone in question.

The preparation of crystals was a sacred practice, laden with symbolism and intention. Before using them, Druids purified them, often bathing them in natural springs, exposing them to moonlight, or burying them in the earth to reconnect with their primordial essence. This ritual of cleansing and consecration was essential to ensure that the energy of the stone was aligned with the desired purpose. Only after this process were the crystals employed in different practices, from healing physical and emotional ailments to protecting against negative forces and channeling messages from the Otherworld. The Druids knew that crystals acted as intermediaries between human beings and cosmic forces, expanding spiritual perception and allowing a deeper contact with the invisible dimensions.

The variety of crystals used by the Celts was vast, each with its specific function within magic and spirituality. Clear quartz, for example, was considered the master healer, an energy amplifier capable of harmonizing the chakras and restoring inner balance. Its purity symbolized the direct connection with the divine, making it indispensable in rituals of purification and spiritual strengthening. For those seeking wisdom and elevation of consciousness, amethyst was the ideal stone. Its violet hue evoked spirituality and introspection, aiding in meditation, calming the mind, and protecting against negative influences. Furthermore, it was considered a powerful ally in combating addictions and destructive patterns, aiding in inner transformation.

Carnelian, on the other hand, was a stone of vibrant energy, associated with vitality, courage, and creativity. Its reddish glow evoked the force of fire, propelling action and dispelling fear. Many Celtic warriors carried carnelian amulets onto the battlefield, believing that it conferred protection and vigor upon them. Turquoise, with its blue-green hue, was revered as a sacred stone, a symbol of good luck and harmony. The Celts believed that it had the power to strengthen bonds of friendship, bring serenity, and facilitate communication with the spiritual world. In addition, it was widely used as a protective talisman against harmful energies and diseases.

For Celtic women, moonstone held a special meaning. Associated with femininity and intuition, it was considered a manifestation of lunar energy and the sacred feminine. It was believed that this stone helped balance emotions, promoted fertility, and attracted true love. Many Celtic priestesses and healers used moonstone in their rituals, seeking to access intuitive wisdom and strengthen their connection with natural forces. Obsidian, with its dark and mysterious appearance, was a stone of protection and transformation. The Celts used it to ward off negative influences, purify environments, and aid in emotional healing. As a mirror of the soul, obsidian brought hidden truths to the surface and helped those seeking self-knowledge and spiritual growth.

In addition to crystals, the Celts also recognized the strength of raw stones found in nature, such as granite, quartzite, and sandstone. These rocks were used in the construction of sacred monuments, such as menhirs, stone circles, and dolmens. Each of these structures had a specific purpose, whether as a point of connection with the earth's energy, a place of rituals, or a passage to the Otherworld. It was believed that these stones possessed an ancestral energy, accumulated over the centuries, and that they could be used for healing, protection, and spiritual guidance.

Stone circles, like the famous Stonehenge, were meticulously planned, respecting astronomical alignments and energy flows of the earth. These places served as true open-air temples, where Druids and initiates performed ceremonies in tune with natural cycles. During the solstices and equinoxes, these sacred spaces were the scene of rituals that sought to balance the forces of nature and renew the harmony between the human world and the divine. For the Celts, stones were not just inert matter, but living entities, charged with power and memory. They guarded the history of the earth and transmitted its wisdom to those who knew how to listen to them.

In essence, the use of crystals and stones in the Celtic tradition reveals a worldview deeply connected to nature and the mysteries of the universe. They did not see minerals as mere objects of value, but as instruments of transformation and enlightenment. Through observation, respect, and interaction with these natural forces, the Celts sought to understand the secrets of the cosmos and find balance in their earthly journey. Today, we can draw inspiration from this ancestral knowledge and integrate the magic of crystals into our own lives, whether through meditation, contemplation, or the conscious use of these precious gifts from the earth.

Crystals and stones, in the Celtic view, were more than just ornaments or ritual tools; they represented the very essence of the earth, concentrating within themselves the memory of the world and the flows of energy that permeate all existence. By recognizing them as spiritual allies, the Celts teach us that nature offers not only beauty, but also wisdom and protection to those who know how to listen to it. Today, as we reclaim this ancestral knowledge, we can rediscover in minerals a path of connection with the sacred, allowing their vibrations to guide us in our search for balance, strength, and harmony with the universe.

Chapter 20
Celtic Divination

The Celtic tradition of divination was based on the belief that the universe was in constant communication with those who knew how to listen to its messages. For these people, time was not linear, but a cycle where past, present, and future intertwined, allowing future events to be intuited from careful observation of the natural and spiritual world. The Celts saw life as a continuous flow of energies and patterns, where each event was linked to invisible forces that could be interpreted by the wise and initiated. Thus, divination was not about predicting an unchanging destiny, but about understanding the trends and possibilities that shaped each individual's journey.

The druids, respected as intermediaries between men and gods, were the main interpreters of these hidden signs. Endowed with vast knowledge about nature and the spiritual world, they dedicated themselves to the study of symbols, patterns and natural manifestations to offer guidance and counsel. Through the observation of the flight of birds, the interpretation of dreams and the reading of elements such as bones and stones, they deciphered omens and helped in making important decisions. Intuition, combined with ancestral knowledge, allowed these wise men to perceive subtleties that escaped most people, transforming divination into a refined and deeply respected art.

More than a mere instrument of prediction, Celtic divination was a means of connection with the sacred and a reflection of the harmonious relationship of these people with nature. Each interpreted sign carried with it not only an answer, but also a teaching about the cycles of life and the interdependence between all things. Respect for omens and the wisdom contained in them guided everything from personal matters to decisions of leaders and entire communities. Thus, this ancient practice was consolidated as one of the pillars of Celtic culture, transmitting, through generations, the importance of being attentive to the messages of the universe and of understanding that destiny, far from being fixed, was a path shaped by the choices and perception of those who knew how to listen to the signs around them.

The druids, masters of divination, were the guardians of hidden mysteries and interpreters of the signs that permeated the natural and spiritual world. Endowed with deep knowledge and sensitivity, they dedicated themselves to the meticulous observation of nature, dreams and omens, seeking to unravel the messages that guided the destiny of individuals and communities. For the Celts, divination was not mere curiosity or superstition, but a sacred link with the universe, a means of understanding the flows and cycles that governed life. Practiced with reverence, this art required concentration, keen intuition, and a deep connection to the invisible forces that shaped reality.

Among the techniques used by druids, some were widely recognized and passed down through generations. Bone reading, for example, consisted of the use of small animal bones, shells or stones engraved with sacred symbols. These elements were thrown onto a surface, and the patterns formed were meticulously analyzed. Each piece carried its own meaning, and the way they fell revealed hidden messages. The position, proximity between the bones and even the direction they pointed were taken into account in the interpretation. It was not a simple method; it required years of practice and a keen eye to perceive the subtleties of the signs presented.

Dream interpretation was also a fundamental practice within the Celtic tradition. It was believed that, during sleep, the soul could wander between worlds and receive messages from the Otherworld - the domain of the gods and ancestral spirits. Dreams were seen as revelations, capable of conveying advice, warnings, or glimpses of the future. Druids, trained in this art, knew how to recognize dream symbols and decipher them accurately. Dreams with water, for example, could represent deep emotions or premonitions related to changes and renewals. Dreams with specific animals carried distinct meanings, depending on the creature sighted and its behavior within the vision. For the Celts, each dream was a riddle to be solved, a portal to the hidden wisdom of the universe.

Another widely used method was the observation of the flight of birds, a practice known as ornithomancy. The Celts believed that birds were messengers of the gods, and each species had a symbolic meaning. A raven crossing the sky could indicate dark omens or the presence of the gods of war, such as Morrigan. An eagle flying over a village could be interpreted as a sign of protection and strong leadership. In addition to the species, the druids observed the direction of flight, the height at which the birds soared, and even their songs. These details were crucial to correctly interpret the warnings of the spiritual world.

Divination with Ogham was another sacred technique among the Celts. This ancient alphabet, composed of strokes that represented sacred trees, was used not only for writing, but also as an oracle. Small wooden wands, engraved with Ogham symbols, were cast or drawn from a leather bag in specific rituals. Each letter had a correspondence with a type of tree and carried deep meanings. For example, the letter "Duir", associated with oak, represented strength, resilience and wisdom, while "Beith", linked to birch, symbolized rebirth and new beginnings. The druids used this method to guide kings, warriors and those seeking answers to important dilemmas.

Nature itself was a vast book of signs and omens for the Celts. Each natural phenomenon was analyzed with attention and respect, as it was believed that the gods spoke through the wind, rain, phases of the moon and animal behavior. A sudden swirl of leaves could be interpreted as the presence of spirits or an imminent change. The early flowering of certain plants could indicate a prosperous season, while untimely storms were seen as warnings from the gods. The moon, in its different phases, also exerted great influence over divination rituals, with the full moon being especially conducive to spiritual practices and revelations.

Celtic divination was not just about trying to predict the future, but about a broader understanding of life and its mysteries. Integrating ancestral knowledge, intuition and a deep connection with the spiritual world, this practice offered guidance and wisdom, helping people make more conscious decisions aligned with the natural flows of the universe. By observing the signs of nature and interpreting their hidden meanings, the druids guided their peoples with discernment and reverence, reminding them that destiny was not a fixed and unchanging path, but a journey shaped by the choices and perceptions of those who knew how to listen to the messages of the cosmos.

In this way, Celtic divination transcended the mere search for answers and was consolidated as a path of connection with the sacred, a continuous dialogue between the visible and the invisible. By interpreting the signs of nature and the omens of the spiritual world, the druids not only assisted in decision-making, but also strengthened the relationship of the Celtic people with the cycles of existence. Each reading, each dream deciphered, each bird flight observed reaffirmed the belief that life was a flow of energies in constant transformation, where true power was not in knowing the future, but in understanding the forces that shaped it.

Chapter 21
Sacred Alphabet

Ogham is much more than an ancient alphabet; it is a system of knowledge deeply rooted in the Celts' connection with nature and the sacred. Each of its strokes represents more than a simple letter—it brings with it the essence of trees, the cycles of life, and the mysteries of the universe. For the Celts, language was not just a means of communication, but a reflection of the natural and spiritual order of the world. Ogham, with its symbolic structure and its link to sacred trees, was a link between men, the earth, and the gods, serving both as a writing tool and as a means of divination and magic.

The relationship between trees and Ogham reveals the importance of the natural world in Celtic cosmology. Each feda, or letter, was associated with a specific tree, and each tree possessed symbolic attributes that guided rituals, beliefs, and spiritual practices. Knowledge of Ogham was not limited to reading and writing; it required a deeper understanding of nature and its cycles. Birch, for example, linked to the first letter Beith, symbolized renewal and new beginnings, while oak, corresponding to Duir, represented strength and ancestral wisdom. In this way, the Celts saw Ogham as a map of knowledge and a means of interpreting the energies that governed life and destiny.

In addition to its linguistic and symbolic importance, Ogham was an essential tool for magic and divination. Druids used wands inscribed with its characters to perform oracular consultations, seeking answers in the combinations of letters that appeared when they were cast or chosen. Each inscription was loaded with meanings, functioning as a bridge between the visible and invisible world. This practice reinforced the Celtic belief in the interconnection between the physical and spiritual planes, allowing initiates to interpret omens and receive guidance from beyond. In this way, Ogham transcended its function as a simple alphabet, becoming a sacred code that reflected the Celts' worldview and their quest for harmony with nature and the mysteries of the universe.

The origin of Ogham is lost in the mists of time, shrouded in myths and legends that have been passed down through generations. Some scholars suggest that it may have evolved from influences of runic alphabets, possibly introduced by Germanic peoples who migrated to the British Isles. Others, however, argue that Ogham arose independently, conceived as a system of sacred writing by the druids themselves. Regardless of its true origin, the fact is that this alphabet was consolidated as an essential tool for the Celts, going far beyond simple communication and assuming a fundamental role in the spiritual, magical and divinatory aspects of Celtic culture.

Originally, Ogham was used to record names, short messages, and inscriptions on stones and monuments. Traces of this use can still be found today in ogham stones scattered throughout Ireland and Great Britain, where vertical and diagonal strokes were carved on the edges of stones to form words. However, this writing was not limited to marking territories or recording events. Its importance transcended practical functionality, being a bridge between the material and spiritual world. It was a sacred language, a code that allowed connection with invisible forces, a means by which the Celts accessed hidden knowledge and interpreted the mysteries of the universe.

Each feda, or letter of Ogham, was intrinsically linked to a specific tree, and each tree carried with it a set of deep symbolic meanings. This association with nature meant that Ogham was not just an alphabet, but a true system of knowledge, reflecting the Celtic perception that the forest was a living organism, endowed with consciousness and wisdom. The first letter, Beith, corresponded to birch, a tree linked to purification and new beginnings. The second, Luis, represented the rowan, a tree associated with protection and overcoming challenges. Thus, each Ogham symbol was not just a linguistic unit, but also an emblem of natural forces that could be invoked and used in rituals, spells, and spiritual practices.

Druids, considered the guardians of this knowledge, used Ogham in a variety of ways, one of the most common being the making of magic wands. Made with the wood corresponding to each letter, these wands were engraved with ogham inscriptions and used in rituals of invocation, protection, and divination. Ash wood, for example, was often chosen for making these wands, as this tree was seen as a link between the earthly and spiritual worlds. Each inscription carried a specific purpose, and by engraving them on the wood, the druids believed they were channeling the energies of the corresponding tree, enhancing the desired effects.

In addition, Ogham was widely used as an oracle. The most common method of divination involved the use of small wooden sticks, each containing a symbol of the alphabet. The druids would cast these sticks onto a cloth or flat surface, observing the position in which they fell and interpreting the letters facing upwards. This reading allowed access to messages and omens, providing guidance for those seeking answers about the future or clarification on important decisions. Each letter had its own meaning, and the combination of letters revealed nuances and developments about the issue analyzed. This divinatory system was widely respected, as it was based on the belief that nature communicated its wisdom in subtle ways, just knowing how to interpret its signs.

Ogham was also used in the creation of amulets and talismans of protection. Small pieces of wood or stones were engraved with specific letters to attract certain energies. For example, someone seeking courage and resilience could carry a talisman with the inscription Duir, corresponding to oak, a tree symbolizing strength and wisdom. For those who needed spiritual protection, the inscription Luis, of the rowan, was a common choice, as it was believed that this tree warded off negative influences and evil spirits.

But Ogham was not just a magical or divinatory tool; it was, above all, a reflection of the Celtic worldview. The deep connection between letters and trees revealed a cyclical understanding of life, in which each feda represented not just an abstract concept, but a stage in the natural and human cycle. Just as trees went through different phases throughout the seasons, individuals also experienced periods of growth, transformation, decline, and renewal. Ogham, therefore, served as a symbolic map to guide the Celts on their spiritual journey, helping them to better understand their role in the universe and to seek balance with the forces of nature.

This understanding of life as a continuous cycle made Ogham an instrument of wisdom and self-knowledge. For the Celts, studying this alphabet was not just about learning a set of symbols and phonemes, but about immersing yourself in a philosophy of life that valued harmony with nature and respect for its rhythms. Even today, Ogham continues to inspire those seeking a deeper connection with the natural world. Its principles can be applied as a tool for meditation, reflection and reconnection with the primordial essence of life. Through contemplation of trees and understanding their symbolic meanings, we can access this ancient Celtic wisdom and use it to enrich our own journey, seeking balance, protection, and spiritual renewal.

The legacy of Ogham lives on as a testament to the Celts' deep relationship with nature and the sacred.

More than an alphabet, it represents a path of knowledge and introspection, a bridge between the visible and the invisible, between man and the mysteries of the universe. Its symbols echo the ancestral wisdom of those who saw trees not only as living beings, but as guardians of secrets and guides on the human journey. Even today, those who set out to study Ogham open themselves to a more intuitive understanding of life, allowing its letters to continue to whisper ancient teachings to those who know how to listen.

Chapter 22
Rituals and Ceremonies

Celtic rituals were sacred celebrations that marked the deep relationship between humans, nature, and the divine. More than just ceremonies, these rites represented moments of spiritual alignment, honoring the cycles of life, the forces of nature, and the presence of the ancestors. Each ritual was a portal to communion with the sacred, establishing a balance between the physical and spiritual world. The Celts believed that everything in existence was interconnected—the rising and setting of the sun, the phases of the moon, the seasons, the growth of crops, and even the individual paths of living beings. Thus, each ceremony carried a greater purpose: to strengthen spiritual bonds, bring protection, and ensure harmony between the visible and invisible realms.

Ritual practices were varied and encompassed all spheres of Celtic life. There were seasonal ceremonies, aligned with the festivals of the sacred calendar, such as Beltane, Samhain, Imbolc, and Lughnasadh, which marked fundamental transitions in the agricultural and spiritual year. There were also rites of passage, which marked important moments in an individual's life, such as births, initiations, marriages, and funerals.

Additionally, rituals of healing, protection, and prosperity were often performed, reinforcing the belief that the energy of the universe could be channeled for personal and community well-being. The environment in which these ceremonies took place was carefully chosen—ancestral forests, riverbanks, sacred hills, and stone circles were considered ideal places to establish this connection with the divine.

Druids, the keepers of spiritual and natural knowledge, played the role of guides in these rituals, conducting invocations, offerings, and enchantments. The participation of the community was essential, as each person contributed their energy and devotion. Elements such as fire, water, herbs, crystals, and sacred symbols were incorporated into ceremonies to amplify the intention of the ritual. The closing was always marked by gestures of gratitude to the gods and ancestors, reaffirming the Celts' respect for cosmic balance. This legacy of connection and reverence for nature remains alive, inspiring those who seek to reclaim ancestral practices and adapt ancient rituals to modern life, strengthening spirituality and self-knowledge through Celtic wisdom.

Celtic rituals were performed in diverse contexts and with varied purposes, each carrying a unique structure and deep meanings, but sharing essential elements that ensured their effectiveness and sacredness. Among the most common were seasonal rituals, celebrated during the festivals of the Celtic calendar, such as Beltane, Samhain, Imbolc, and Lughnasadh, which marked crucial moments in the agricultural and spiritual cycle. In addition to these, rites of passage marked significant events in the individual journey, such as births, initiations, marriages, and funerals. Specific rituals were also performed for healing, protection, prosperity, and divination, all based on the belief that it was possible to channel universal energies to promote personal and collective well-being.

Preparation for the ritual was considered essential, as it not only created an environment conducive to the manifestation of the sacred, but also helped participants enter the proper state of consciousness to establish a genuine connection with the divine. The location of the ritual was chosen with great care, always taking into account its relationship with the natural elements and the spiritual forces present there. Many rituals took place in clearings of ancestral forests, on the banks of sacred rivers, on hills, or within stone circles, spaces charged with energy and history. However, rituals could also be performed in the home itself, as long as the environment was properly prepared to receive the sacred.

The first step in preparing the space was its purification. This process varied according to local tradition and the purpose of the ritual, but generally involved the use of burning herbs, such as sage, mugwort, or juniper, whose purifying properties helped ward off negative influences and balance the energies of the environment. In addition to fumigation, the scattering of consecrated water around the space and the use of sacred symbols drawn on the ground, such as the triskele or the Celtic spiral, were common ways to delimit and protect the site.

At the center of the sacred space, an altar was set up to serve as the focal point of the ceremony. This altar contained symbolic elements carefully chosen to reinforce the intention of the ritual. Candles were lit to represent the sacred fire and illuminate the spiritual path. Incense was burned to lift prayers and intentions to the gods and ancestors. Flowers and crystals were arranged to harmonize the energy of the environment, while offerings were prepared as a demonstration of respect and gratitude to the spiritual world. These elements varied according to the purpose of the ritual, but their presence was essential to create a link between the physical and the ethereal.

Invocation was one of the most important moments of the ritual, as it was when the participants called upon the divine forces and ancestors to participate in the ceremony. This stage could be carried out through chants, dances, poems, and enchantments, all designed to intensify the connection with the spirits and open a channel of communication with the invisible world. Druids, as spiritual guides, led this part of the ritual, chanting sacred words and guiding the participants to focus their energy and intention. Each movement, each word spoken or sung, had a deep meaning, serving as a means to achieve the desired attunement with the universe.

Offerings were another fundamental aspect of the ritual, representing not only a gesture of gratitude but also an act of reciprocity between the human world and the spiritual world. The Celts believed that by offering something of value, they strengthened their connection with the gods and secured their blessings. The items offered varied according to the type of ritual and could include food, such as bread and honey; beverages, such as mead and milk; herbs and flowers harvested at auspicious times; energized crystals; and even objects of personal value. In some cases, participants dedicated their own time and energy as a form of offering, performing acts of devotion and committing themselves to following a spiritual path aligned with the forces invoked.

Throughout the ceremony, the energy generated by the group intensified, creating an environment charged with vibration and spiritual power. Depending on the purpose of the ritual, specific practices could be incorporated, such as reading omens by observing the flames of candles, the flight of birds, or the arrangement of fallen leaves in the wind. In healing rituals, medicinal herbs were consecrated and applied to the sick, while words of power were spoken to restore physical and spiritual balance. In protection rituals, magic circles were drawn, and amulets were blessed to protect participants from harmful influences.

The closing of the ritual was a time of gratitude and farewell to the spiritual forces invoked. The participants thanked the gods and ancestors for their presence and for the blessings received, recognizing the importance of the energy exchange that had taken place. The candles were extinguished with respect, symbolizing the return to the everyday world, and the altar was dismantled with due reverence. The ritual site was left in order, as a form of respect for nature and the spirits of the place, ensuring that harmony was maintained even after the ceremony ended.

Celtic rituals and ceremonies were, above all, living expressions of the spirituality of these people, reflecting their worldview, their relationship with nature, and their search for the sacred. They were moments of deep connection with the forces that governed life, celebrations of existence, and opportunities for personal transformation. By understanding these ancestral practices, we can be inspired by them and adapt them to our reality, creating our own rituals to strengthen our spirituality and cultivate a greater sense of harmony and balance in our journey.

Throughout the centuries, Celtic rituals have remained as testimonies to the deep wisdom of these people, echoing a sacred connection with the universe and its natural cycles. More than just traditions, these ceremonies were living expressions of the belief that existence was a continuous flow of energies, where each ritualistic gesture strengthened the bonds between the visible and invisible worlds. Even today, by rescuing and adapting these ancient teachings, it is possible to rediscover a path of authentic spirituality, where harmony with nature and respect for ancestral forces continue to guide those who seek meaning and balance in their journeys.

Chapter 23
Creating a Celtic Altar

Setting up a Celtic altar is an act of deep connection with spirituality, a sacred space that reflects the relationship between the individual, nature, and the mysteries of the universe. More than just an arrangement of objects, an altar is a physical manifestation of the intentions, beliefs, and devotion of the one who creates it. In the Celtic world, sacredness was perceived in all aspects of existence, and the creation of an altar represented an extension of this principle, allowing a focal point for rituals, meditations, and offerings to the gods and ancestors. The careful choice of each element inserted in the altar not only strengthens the spiritual connection but also channels energies that harmonize and protect the surrounding environment.

Unlike other spiritual traditions with strict rules about the arrangement of sacred elements, the Celtic altar is highly personal and adaptable, reflecting the spiritual journey of the one who builds it. Still, certain principles can be followed to enhance its strength and meaning. The location of the altar should be chosen with intuition and respect, favoring a quiet environment where energy flows freely. It can be indoors, occupying a special shelf, a corner of the bedroom or living room, or it can be set up outdoors, in gardens, balconies, or amidst nature, reinforcing the ancestral connection of the Celts with the natural elements. Once the location is determined, sacred objects can be arranged to represent the balance of cosmic forces, with symbols that refer to the four elements—earth, air, fire, and water—and to the deities or energies that one wishes to invoke.

More than just a static structure, the Celtic altar should be a living space, constantly renewed and used. Lit candles, burning incense, and the regular exchange of offerings keep the energy active and the connection always present. Elements such as stones, Celtic symbols, images of deities, and personal objects charged with meaning can be incorporated, making the altar a unique representation of its creator's spirituality. This space is not only a place for rituals or prayers but a refuge where it is possible to reconnect with the sacred at any time of the day. Thus, building and caring for a Celtic altar is not only a gesture of devotion but an ongoing commitment to harmony between the physical and spiritual world, bringing the essence of Celtic tradition into everyday life in a profound and meaningful way.

Setting up a Celtic altar is an act of deep connection with spirituality, a reflection of the bond between the individual and nature, a sacred space where intentions, devotions, and energies are manifested. Unlike more rigid spiritual traditions, where the arrangement of sacred elements follows specific rules, the Celtic altar is a personal expression, adaptable to the tastes, beliefs, and circumstances of the one who builds it. However, for this altar to become a point of power and harmony, some essential elements can be incorporated, ensuring that it resonates with the essence of Celtic tradition.

The first step in creating a Celtic altar is to choose a suitable location, a space that promotes spiritual connection and tranquility. This place can be indoors, such as a private corner of the bedroom, a special shelf in the living room, or even a space in the office. If possible, an outdoor altar can further intensify this connection with the natural elements and can be set up in the garden, on the balcony, or under the canopy of a tree. The most important thing is that the location is meaningful to the one who uses it, providing an environment of serenity and introspection.

With the space chosen, the assembly of the altar begins, and one of the first elements to consider is the base on which the sacred objects will be placed. A special cloth can be used to cover the surface, creating a symbolic foundation for the other elements. This fabric can be green, evoking the fertility and vitality of the earth; blue, referring to the sacred waters and the spiritual world; brown, representing the connection with ancestral roots; or even contain Celtic patterns and symbols, such as spirals, intertwined knots, and geometric patterns that reflect the cycles of life.

To harmonize the altar with the forces of nature, it is essential to include representations of the four elements. The earth can be symbolized by crystals, natural stones, or small pots of plants, bringing the stability and energy of fertile soil. Air can be represented by a feather, incense that spreads its fragrance through the environment, or even a wind chime, whose subtle melody invokes the presence of the element. Fire, in turn, can be present in the form of candles, whose flame symbolizes transformation and spiritual light, or even through solar symbols, such as golden discs or images of the sun. Water can be represented by a shell, a chalice with pure water, or even a small container containing river, sea, or rainwater, evoking fluidity and intuition.

In addition to these natural elements, Celtic symbols play a fundamental role in the composition of the altar. The Celtic knot, with its continuous interweaving, represents the interconnection of life and eternity. The triskele, with its three spirals, symbolizes the cycles of existence, such as birth, life, and death, or body, mind, and spirit. The Celtic cross, marked by the circle that joins its arms, reflects the fusion between the sacred and the earthly, and the simple spiral refers to the individual journey of spiritual growth. These symbols can be incorporated into the altar in the form of talismans, sculptures, engravings, or even drawn directly on the fabric that covers the base.

If there is a particular connection with any Celtic deity, it is interesting to include a representation of this sacred presence. It can be a statuette, an illustration, or even an object that refers to the chosen deity. Each Celtic god and goddess has specific attributes: Brigid, for example, is associated with inspiration, healing, and blacksmithing; Cernunnos, with the natural world and fertility; Dagda, with abundance and ancestral knowledge. By bringing these images to the altar, a focal point of veneration and strengthening of the connection with divine energies is created.

Another essential aspect of the Celtic altar is the practice of offerings. This gesture represents gratitude, reverence, and reciprocity with the spiritual world. Small gifts can be placed on the altar as a way of honoring the gods and ancestors: fresh flowers, which symbolize renewal; fruits, which evoke prosperity; grains and seeds, representing fertility and continuity; incense and candles, which elevate prayers and intentions to the universe. These items should be renewed periodically, demonstrating respect and commitment to maintaining sacred energy.

Although these traditional elements exist, personalization of the altar is encouraged, making it an authentic expression of the spiritual journey of the one who builds it. Photographs of loved ones can be included, strengthening the bond with ancestors. Personal objects that have special meaning, such as stones found on walks, shells brought from trips, or family artifacts, can add layers of memory and energy to the space. Books that inspire spiritual practice, specific crystals for protection and harmony, or small magical artifacts can also be incorporated, as long as they resonate with the purpose of the altar.

Maintaining the altar is a fundamental part of this process. Keeping it clean and organized ensures that the energy concentrated there remains fluid and vibrant. Objects can be regularly cleaned with a damp cloth or fumigated with herbs, such as sage or rosemary, for purification. The offerings must be renewed, and the exchange of elements can occur according to the seasons, reflecting the natural cycle and adjusting the altar to the predominant energy of each period. Also, lighting candles and incense regularly helps keep the space active and charged with good vibrations.

More than just a decorative arrangement, a Celtic altar is a meeting point between the visible and the invisible, a space where one can meditate, pray, reflect, and reconnect with the sacred. Whether as a place for formal rituals or simply as a refuge for moments of introspection, it becomes a physical representation of Celtic spirituality in everyday life. Creating and caring for this altar is a gesture of respect for ancestral traditions, a commitment to harmony between the material and spiritual world, and a way of bringing the magic of Celtic culture into one's own life.

Thus, the Celtic altar becomes more than just a physical space—it is a reflection of the spiritual journey of the one who builds it, a link between past and present, between the sacred and the everyday. By nurturing it with intentions, offerings, and moments of contemplation, it remains alive, vibrant, and aligned with the energies of the universe. Whether to honor the gods, strengthen the connection with nature, or simply find a refuge of peace, this altar is an invitation to experience Celtic spirituality in an authentic and transformative way, bringing the wisdom and magic of the ancients into everyday life.

Chapter 24
Celebrating the Festivals

Celtic festivals were sacred celebrations that marked the passage of time and reflected the deep connection of these people with the natural cycles. Each festival was a moment of renewal and transformation, in which the earth, the gods, and the ancestors were honored, recognizing the interdependence between all forms of life. These celebrations not only accompanied the rhythm of the seasons but also symbolized the cycles of human existence—birth, growth, maturity, and renewal. Through rituals, offerings, feasts, and dances, the Celts strengthened their connection with the spiritual world, seeking guidance, protection, and blessings for the future.

The Celtic sacred calendar was composed of eight main festivals, divided between solar festivals and fire festivals. The solar festivals—the solstices and equinoxes—celebrated the changes in light and darkness throughout the year, symbolizing the balance between opposing forces. The fire festivals—Imbolc, Beltane, Lughnasadh, and Samhain—marked key moments in the agricultural and spiritual cycle, being occasions to plant intentions, strengthen community ties, and pay homage to the gods and spirits of nature. Each festival had its own practices and meanings, but all shared the principle of respect for the cycles of life and the understanding that time was not linear, but cyclical, repeating itself in patterns that guided existence.

The celebration of these festivals did not require a fixed structure, but rather the openness to feel and honor the energy of each moment. Rituals could be performed individually or in groups, with symbolic offerings, dances around bonfires, meditations, and sacred chants. Gratitude for the abundance received and reflection on inner transformations were essential elements of these celebrations. Today, rescuing these festivals means more than just following ancient traditions; it is an act of reconnection with nature and its cycles, allowing each person to find their own rhythm and walk with more awareness and balance through the journey of life.

Celebrating Celtic festivals does not require adherence to dogmas or rigid rules, but rather an authentic and meaningful experience, shaped by the beliefs, preferences, and possibilities of each person. The essential thing is to be open to feeling the energy of each celebration, honoring the natural cycles, and recognizing the sacredness of life in all its phases. This connection does not need to follow a strict format, as its true essence lies in the intention and attunement to the rhythms of the universe.

To properly prepare for these celebrations, it is important to begin by understanding the meaning of each festival. This involves exploring its origin, the associated deities, symbols, and traditional practices. Knowledge about each festival allows not only a more authentic experience, but also a deeper connection with the energy it carries. Reading about myths, stories, and associated rituals can enrich understanding and awaken a sense of belonging to this ancestral tradition.

Creating a suitable space for the celebration is another important step. This space can be an altar inside the house, a garden, or a place in nature, and should be purified and decorated according to the symbolism of the festival. Elements such as candles, crystals, flowers, and fruits can be used to represent the season and the spiritual aspects of the festival. If possible, choosing an outdoor location, where it is possible to feel the wind, hear the sounds of the earth, and observe the sky, can amplify the connection with natural energies.

Preparation for festivals also involves a direct connection with nature. Walking through woods, fields, or beaches, feeling the ground beneath your feet, perceiving the subtle changes of the season, and observing the cycles of life around you are ways to align yourself with natural rhythms. This contact allows for a greater perception of the interdependence between all forms of life and reinforces the central idea of Celtic festivals: harmony with the flow of existence.

Purifying the body and mind before the celebration is also an essential aspect. A bath with herbs such as lavender, rosemary, or sage can help cleanse energies and create a state of receptivity. Practices such as meditation, conscious breathing, or even a stretching session can help connect with your inner self, preparing you to absorb the energies of the moment in a deeper and more meaningful way.

At the time of celebration, creating a personalized ritual can be a powerful way to connect with the energy of the festival. This ritual may include lighting candles, burning herbs as an offering to the gods and ancestors, reciting prayers or chants, meditating on the meanings of the festival, and even practicing sacred dances around a bonfire. The important thing is that each gesture carries intention and reverence.

Sharing this experience with others can make it even more special. If possible, gathering friends and family who share this connection can strengthen bonds and make the celebration more vibrant. Preparing a feast with seasonal foods, telling stories, singing, or performing collective rituals are ways to honor the energy of the festivity in a community way.

Gratitude is a fundamental element in any Celtic celebration. Giving thanks for the abundance of the earth, for the blessings received, and for the experiences lived throughout the previous cycle strengthens the connection with the universe and opens the way for the continuity of the flow of prosperity. Expressing this gratitude can be done in many ways: through words, offerings, symbolic gestures, or even the simple act of contemplation.

Each festival marks a transition within the great cycle of life, and reflecting on this movement is an essential part of the celebration. Observing the lessons learned, identifying patterns that need to be transformed, and setting intentions for the next cycle allows each festival to also be a time of personal growth and renewal.

Adapting festivals to each person's reality is a legitimate and necessary practice. It will not always be possible to follow traditions exactly as they were performed in antiquity, but this does not diminish the depth of the experience. Creativity can be used to create your own rituals, adapt symbolic elements to the environment in which you live, and incorporate practices that have personal meaning.

Honoring one's own ancestry is another aspect that can enrich the celebration. For those who have roots in different cultures, it is possible to integrate elements of these traditions into Celtic festivals, creating a respectful and authentic fusion. After all, the spirit of these festivities lies in the connection with natural cycles, something that transcends any specific tradition and can be experienced in many ways.

Above all, celebrating Celtic festivals is celebrating life. It is an invitation to recognize the magic that permeates everyday life, to live with more awareness and gratitude, and to strengthen the connection with the earth, with ancestors, and with one's own being. Regardless of how one chooses to celebrate, the most important thing is to keep alive the flame of respect for the cycles of nature and allow this connection to illuminate the path throughout life's journey.

Celtic festivals are not just seasonal events, but opportunities to align with the rhythms of the universe and celebrate the interconnection between all things. By bringing these ancient rituals into the present, whether individually or collectively, we reaffirm our connection to the earth, to our ancestors, and to the very essence of existence. Each celebration is a reminder that we are part of a larger cycle, where renewal and transformation go hand in hand, inviting us to live with more presence, gratitude, and respect for the mysteries of life.

Chapter 25
Meditation and Connection

Celtic meditation is a profound journey of self-knowledge and connection with the sacred, rooted in the harmony between human beings and nature. Unlike a simple relaxation practice, it is a spiritual path that rescues ancestral wisdom and strengthens ties with the natural cycles of life. In its essence, it is not just an exercise to calm the mind, but a sensory and mystical experience that awakens awareness to the interconnectedness of all things.

For the Celts, everything in nature was endowed with life and spirituality—from the wind that blew through the woods to the waters that flowed through the streams. Thus, meditation was not seen as a withdrawal from the external world, but rather as a means of immersing oneself deeply in it, absorbing its energy and subtle messages. The practitioner learned to listen to the voice of the wind, feel the pulse of the earth beneath their feet, and recognize the flow of life that permeates each leaf, each raindrop, each star in the night sky. In this way, meditation became a bridge between the visible and invisible domains, allowing those who practiced it to tune in to the wisdom of their ancestors and the presence of the gods.

Over the centuries, this practice has been passed down from generation to generation, preserving techniques that involve visualizations, chanting, and contemplation of nature. Unlike Eastern meditative traditions, which often seek to empty the mind, the Celtic approach values the active experience of imagination and energetic connection. Inner silence is not a goal in itself, but a state that allows one to perceive the subtle communication between the physical and spiritual world. Through this practice, the Celts found guidance for their journeys, strengthened their intuition, and developed a sense of belonging to the great flow of existence. It was believed that, by meditating, it was possible to access not only one's own inner essence, but also the energies of the earth, rivers, trees, and stars. Thus, each meditative practice was shaped by the surrounding environment, becoming unique and deeply personal. The forest, for example, offered a space for introspection and listening, while the bank of a river facilitated emotional fluidity and the renewal of energies. In this way, the act of meditating became a sacred ritual of connection and spiritual strengthening.

By incorporating this practice into everyday life, the individual not only benefited from the serenity and mental clarity that meditation provided but also expanded their perception of their own existence. The world was no longer seen only with the physical eyes but began to be understood also through the spiritual senses. Each meditative moment became an opportunity for learning and alignment with the forces that govern the universe. The regularity of this practice not only enhanced intuition and creativity but also awakened a deep respect for nature and the balance it offers. Celtic meditation, therefore, was not just an isolated moment of internalization, but a way of life that taught one to walk consciously and harmoniously through the world. By opening the heart and mind to this connection, the practitioner not only found inner peace but also became a living link in the great web of existence, understanding that each being, each element of nature, and each cycle of life is part of an interconnected and sacred whole.

Celtic meditation stands out among spiritual practices for its emphasis on the deep connection with nature and the invisible world that permeates it. Unlike Eastern meditative traditions, which often seek to empty the mind to achieve states of contemplation, the Celtic approach values the active experience of the senses, inviting the practitioner to fill the mind with images, sounds, and sensations. It is an immersion in the energy of the gods, the wisdom of the ancestors, and the life force that runs through all that exists. It is a dynamic meditation, which is not limited to internalization, but seeks to integrate body, mind, and spirit in perfect harmony with the elements of nature.

There are several techniques that can be applied within Celtic meditation, each providing a specific type of spiritual connection. One of the most fundamental is nature meditation, which consists of finding a quiet and inspiring place outdoors—a serene forest, a flower garden, the bank of a river, or even the top of a mountain. Upon settling comfortably in this environment, the practitioner closes their eyes and directs their attention to the breath, allowing it to become slow and deep. From this point, the mind opens to full sensory perception: the subtle sounds of the wind whispering through the leaves, the distant singing of birds, the gentle rhythm of water running over stones. The body attunes itself to the warmth of the sun warming the skin, the texture of the earth beneath the feet, the coolness of the air filling the lungs. In this immersion, the practitioner allows the energy of the environment to envelop them, nourishing their essence and bringing balance and healing.

Another powerful practice is visualization meditation, which transports consciousness to a sacred space within the Celtic imaginary. The practitioner, upon closing their eyes, evokes the image of a circle of ancestral stones, a grove of ancient oak trees, or a crystalline fountain whose waters radiate purity and vitality. They focus on the details of this spiritual environment: the vibrant colors of the leaves, the soft glow of the moon filtered through the branches, the scent of wild herbs. Gradually, they feel the energy of this sacred place filling their being, restoring their strength and bringing profound messages. In many cases, visualization leads to encounters with spiritual guides—Celtic gods, ancestral spirits, or power animals. This contact can offer guidance, transmit healing, or simply awaken a sense of belonging to the greater flow of existence. The important thing in this practice is to remain receptive, allowing messages to arrive naturally, whether through images, words, or feelings.

In addition to visualization, another essential technique of Celtic meditation involves the use of mantras and sacred chants. These chants can be done aloud or mentally and are used to awaken consciousness and attune the practitioner to the vibration of the universe. The words, often in the Celtic language, carry within them an ancestral power that resonates in the body and soul. By repeating a mantra or a traditional chant, the practitioner feels the vibrations propagating internally, harmonizing their energy with the melody of the cosmos. This practice is especially useful for those who wish to raise their vibrational frequency, cleanse negative energies, and strengthen their spiritual connection.

Another fascinating approach within Celtic meditation is that which is based on the festivals of the Wheel of the Year. Each of the eight seasonal festivals has a specific energy, reflecting the natural cycles of growth, maturation, gathering, and renewal. The practitioner can meditate on the meaning of each celebration, visualizing the rituals and symbols associated with them. For example, during Samhain, a time when the veil between worlds is thinnest, meditation can focus on contact with ancestors and the closing of cycles. At the summer solstice, the practice can focus on absorbing solar energy and strengthening vitality. By aligning with these seasonal forces, the meditator learns to flow with the rhythms of nature and to better understand their own personal journey.

The benefits of Celtic meditation are vast and encompass all aspects of being. On the physical level, the practice reduces stress and anxiety, as it calms the mind and regulates the production of cortisol, the hormone responsible for stress responses. Deep breathing and attunement with nature promote deep relaxation, which positively impacts the health of the body. In the mental field, meditation strengthens concentration and focus, making it easier to maintain mindfulness in daily tasks. In addition, it stimulates creativity and intuition, allowing the practitioner to have insights and find innovative solutions to the challenges they face.

On the spiritual level, Celtic meditation reinforces the connection with nature and the sacred, helping the practitioner to feel part of a greater whole. By establishing a deep bond with the earth, rivers, trees, and cycles of the universe, they awaken an expanded awareness of their existence and life purpose. This awakening leads to a deeper self-knowledge, allowing them to better understand their gifts, challenges, and paths to follow.

By integrating this practice into everyday life, the meditator realizes that spiritual connection is not restricted to isolated moments of introspection, but can permeate their entire journey. Walking through a field can become a meditation, feeling the breeze on your face can be a call to contemplation, listening to the rustling of leaves can become a whisper of the gods. In this way, Celtic meditation is not just an exercise, but a way of life that teaches you to see the world with more attentive eyes, to listen to the signs of nature, and to understand that each element around you is a reflection of the divine.

To incorporate this practice into one's personal spirituality is to open oneself to the wisdom of the ancient Celts, allowing one's consciousness to expand, one's energy to align with natural rhythms, and the primordial magic of the universe to reveal itself in every aspect of existence.

Celtic meditation is revealed as a portal to a more connected, conscious, and harmonious life. By integrating this practice into everyday life, the individual not only finds balance and inner clarity but also strengthens their relationship with natural cycles and ancestral wisdom. Each moment of contemplation becomes an opportunity for learning, each breath a link with the sacred. In this way, the meditative journey transcends the isolated act and transforms into a continuous path of growth, allowing Celtic spirituality to live not only in the mind but in the very rhythm of existence.

Chapter 26
Working with the Elements

Understanding and working with the elements are fundamental pillars of Celtic spirituality, reflecting the intimate connection between humans and the natural world. The Celts perceived the universe as a great living web, where everything was interconnected and depended on the harmony between the four elements: Earth, Air, Fire, and Water. These elements were not just abstract forces, but tangible and spiritual manifestations of the primordial energy that sustains life. Each carried specific attributes that influenced nature, seasonal cycles, human behavior, and even mystical events. For the Celts, aligning with these forces meant living in balance, respecting nature, and understanding their own role within this cosmic order. Thus, the study of the elements was not limited to theoretical knowledge, but was a daily practice, expressed in rituals, healing, divination, and everyday magic.

The relationship with the elements went beyond simple observation; it was a bond of reciprocity and reverence. The Earth represented the foundation, stability, and nourishment, being honored through cultivation, the building of homes, and respect for the sacred ground of the ancestors. Air symbolized inspiration and intellect, manifesting in the breath of life, the song of the bards, and the wisdom shared among the druids. Fire, the force of transformation, guided courage and passion, reflected in the hearths that warmed homes and the sacred bonfires lit at festivals such as Beltane and Samhain. Water, the source of intuition and purification, was revered in rivers, lakes, and springs, places considered portals between worlds. Each element was associated with gods and spirits, which could be invoked in rituals for protection, guidance, or healing. The Celts believed that by balancing the four elements within themselves, a person achieved physical, mental, and spiritual harmony, becoming more receptive to the energies of the universe.

Practical work with the elements required sensitivity and respect, as each had its own energy flow that needed to be understood. Earth taught patience and prosperity; Air, clarity and communication; Fire, strength and renewal; Water, fluidity and healing. The Celts balanced these forces through seasonal rites, offerings, and meditative practices, recognizing that any excess or deficiency could affect individual and collective well-being. For them, elemental harmony was not a distant concept, but a vital principle that influenced everything from harvests to personal decisions. Working with the elements was, therefore, a way of strengthening not only magic and spirituality, but also the connection with the deepest essence of life. By bringing this wisdom to the present, we can learn to cultivate a more balanced relationship with nature and ourselves, honoring the ancestral legacy that teaches us to live with awareness, respect, and gratitude for the world around us.

The Earth, solid and welcoming, sustains life on its fertile surface, providing the foundation for everything that grows and develops. It represents the materialization of dreams and the stability that maintains the balance of existence. By connecting with the Earth, it is possible to feel its ancestral strength, the same that nourishes ancient forests, green hills, and cultivated fields. Walking barefoot on the ground allows you to absorb its silent energy, while hugging a tree creates a deep bond with its roots, feeling the pulse of life that runs through its trunk. Cultivating a garden is another way to honor this element, participating in the natural cycle of birth, growth, and renewal. Likewise, the connection with stones and crystals makes it possible to access the ancient wisdom contained in the bowels of the world, where the secrets of the Earth are kept. Honoring this element is not just about physical interactions, but also involves respect for the environment. Sustainable practices, such as recycling, planting trees, and adopting conscious habits, are ways of expressing gratitude for everything the Earth offers. After all, harmony with this element reflects the relationship of respect and reciprocity that we must cultivate with the planet.

Air, invisible and subtle, carries within itself the essence of inspiration and thought. It travels through free spaces, carrying with it stories, knowledge, and ideas. It represents freedom, creativity, and transformation, qualities that drive intellectual and spiritual growth. Connecting with Air means allowing yourself to breathe deeply, absorbing its vital energy and letting thoughts flow clearly. Meditating outdoors, feeling the breeze caress your skin, helps you tune in to its ethereal nature. Singing, dancing, and writing are expressions that channel its strength, allowing communication to become an authentic reflection of the inner being. Each word spoken or written carries the mark of Air, transmitting feelings and ideas through its fluidity. Honoring this element means constantly seeking knowledge, exploring new perspectives, and keeping an open mind to learning. Expressing the truth with clarity and honesty is another way to tune in to its energy, as Air teaches that sincere communication is a path to personal and collective evolution.

Fire, ardent and vibrant, manifests itself as the flame that warms, illuminates, and transforms. It represents the passion that drives life, the courage that faces challenges, and the strength that transcends barriers. This element is the symbol of will and action, capable of provoking profound changes when directed with wisdom. To connect with Fire, simply observe its presence in dancing flames, feel its warmth near a bonfire, or light a candle with intention. Movement also awakens this energy; dancing intensely, practicing physical exercise, or simply indulging in activities that bring enthusiasm are ways of honoring the inner Fire. Singing with passion, expressing feelings with fervor, and acting with determination are manifestations of its essence. Honoring Fire means acting with integrity, keeping the flame of truth burning even in the face of difficulties. It teaches that transformation occurs through commitment and courage, and that each action taken with purpose shapes destiny.

Water, fluid and serene, carries in its currents the mystery of intuition and renewal. Its tides dance in tune with the Moon, reflecting the natural rhythm of existence. It represents emotions that flow freely, the sensitivity that perceives the invisible, and the ability to adapt to circumstances. Connecting with Water involves moments of introspection and purification. Taking a relaxing bath, allowing the water to wash away accumulated tension, is a simple but powerful ritual. Swimming in rivers, lakes, or the sea strengthens this connection, allowing you to feel its refreshing and renewing embrace. Meditating near a water source or simply listening to the sound of a stream can bring emotional clarity and tranquility. Honoring this element means accepting one's own emotions, allowing them to flow without repression, and trusting intuition as a guide for life's decisions. Just as water finds its way around obstacles, emotional balance is revealed when one learns to flow with life's challenges, rather than resist them.

The balance between the elements is essential for the harmony of body, mind, and spirit. The Celts believed that when one of the elements was out of balance, this was reflected in health and well-being. The lack of Earth's stability could result in insecurity and lack of direction. Excess Air could cause dispersion and difficulty concentrating. Fire, when uncontrolled, could lead to impulsiveness and exhaustion. Water, in excess, could make emotions overwhelming and paralyzing. To restore this harmony, they used practices such as meditation, specific rituals, the use of herbs and enchantments. Each element could be strengthened or softened as needed, bringing the necessary balance to life. Understanding this dynamic allows us, even today, to adjust our own energies, observing which aspect of our life needs more attention and connection with a certain element. Thus, by consciously working with the forces of nature, we can awaken our inner power, promote healing, and align our existence with the natural cycles of the universe.

By recognizing and integrating the elements into our daily lives, we rescue an ancestral wisdom that teaches us to live in tune with the natural world and with our own essence. The connection with the Earth strengthens us, the Air inspires us, the Fire drives us, and the Water purifies us, forming a continuous cycle of learning and transformation. Honoring these elements is not just a spiritual act, but a commitment to life in its most authentic expression. When we open ourselves to this harmony, we discover that the secrets of nature have always been within us, waiting to be awakened.

Chapter 27
Magic with the Moon

Since time immemorial, the Moon has exerted a magical influence on Earth and its inhabitants, being revered as a symbol of mystery, intuition, and transformation. For the Celts, the Moon was not just a celestial body in the night sky, but a living and sacred entity, a reflection of divine feminine energy and the eternal dance of natural cycles. Its silvery glow illuminated the paths of magic, guiding those who sought to understand the hidden mysteries of existence. Through the observation of the lunar phases, the Celts harmonized their spiritual practices with the rhythms of nature, using the power of the Moon to enhance spells, rituals, and healing processes. It was believed that each lunar phase carried a unique vibration, capable of influencing not only the physical world, but also emotions, dreams, and spirituality. In this way, the connection with the Moon transcended mere astronomical contemplation, becoming a sacred link between humans and the cosmos.

The Celts' relationship with the Moon was deeply rooted in their cyclical view of time and life. Just as the seasons marked the sacred festivals of the Wheel of the Year, the lunar phases determined the most propitious moments for different types of rituals. During the New Moon, the veil between worlds became more subtle, favoring new intentions and the beginning of spiritual projects. As the Crescent Moon advanced in the sky, its energy of growth and expansion strengthened desires and actions, helping to materialize plans and strengthen willpower. At the Full Moon, when its brightness peaked, magical energy became more intense, ideal for rituals of manifestation, love, and fertility. On the other hand, the Waning Moon guided introspection and the closing of cycles, while the Black Moon, a mysterious period of transition, was associated with contact with ancestors and preparation for a new cycle. This knowledge was passed down from generation to generation, preserved by the druids and practitioners of the old faith, who saw in the Moon a powerful ally for magic and self-knowledge.

By incorporating lunar energy into their daily lives, the Celts learned to flow with the cycles of nature and to respect the right time for each action. They understood that everything in life has its own rhythm—a time to be born, grow, shine, diminish, and be reborn. This perception not only strengthened their magic, but also promoted a deep balance between body, mind, and spirit. In modern times, rescuing this connection with the Moon allows us to access ancestral wisdom and bring more harmony to our personal journey. By working with the lunar phases, we can awaken our inner power, align our desires with the energies of the universe, and understand that we are part of a larger cosmic flow. The Moon continues to shine in the sky, just as it always has for the ancient Celts, reminding us that magic is always within our reach, just tune in to its rhythm and allow its light to guide us.

Each lunar phase carried within itself a deep meaning and a unique energy, serving as a compass for the Celts on their magical journey. By understanding and attuning to these cycles, they were able to direct their rituals with greater efficiency, manifesting intentions according to the natural flow of the universe.

On the New Moon, when the sky was enveloped in darkness and the Moon was not yet visible, the Celts saw an invitation to new beginnings. This was the perfect time to plant the seeds of dreams and set intentions for a new cycle. Just as fertile land awaits the arrival of the seed, the energy of the New Moon offered the ideal ground to nurture desires, projects, and inner changes. Purification rituals were often performed during this period, with herbal baths and fumigation using mugwort, lavender, or white sage to cleanse stagnant energies and open paths to new possibilities. In addition, the writing of intentions on scrolls, later burned in sacred flames, was a common practice, symbolizing the commitment to the new cycle that was beginning.

As the Moon began to grow in the sky, its energy propelled movement and expansion. The Crescent Moon represented the period of strengthening the projects initiated on the New Moon, a time to act with determination and courage. The Celts understood that everything in nature followed a gradual process of development, and therefore this was the ideal time to take concrete steps towards the goals set. Prosperity rituals were often performed, including the consecration of coins and grains as symbols of abundance and growth. Herbs such as basil and rosemary were used in infusions and baths to attract luck and protection. In addition, attraction spells were cast, especially those aimed at love and harmony in relationships, using red candles and rose quartz energized by moonlight.

When the Moon reached its maximum splendor, pouring its silvery light over the earth, magic became more intense. The Full Moon was seen as the culmination of all the energies worked on until then, being a time of celebration, gratitude, and deep connection with spirituality. The Celts took advantage of this phase for rituals of love, fertility, and intuition, as they believed that the Full Moon amplified emotions and sensory perception. In sacred groves, groups gathered to dance and sing under the moonlight, evoking the Goddess in her fullness and asking for blessings and protection. Amulets were energized by moonlight, especially stones such as selenite and moonstone, which carried the mystical vibration of this period. In addition, the practice of meditation and lucid dreaming was encouraged, as it was believed that the Full Moon opened portals to the unconscious and to contact with spiritual guides.

With the arrival of the Waning Moon, energy began to withdraw, inviting introspection and detachment. This was the time of liberation, ideal for ending cycles, warding off negative energies, and preparing for the new cycle that would come with the next New Moon. The Celts used this phase for banishing rituals, in which they wrote on sheets of paper everything they wanted to eliminate from their lives and then burned them in ritual bonfires or threw them into rivers so that the water would carry away everything that no longer served them. Lavender and rue were herbs often used in fumigation for energy cleansing, and Epsom salt baths were recommended to discharge accumulated impurities. In addition, this period favored emotional healing, promoting moments of solitude and reflection, in which one sought to understand harmful patterns and transform them.

Finally, there was the Black Moon, a mysterious and silent interval in the three days preceding the New Moon. This was a sacred time of retreat, a period of deep connection with the unconscious and with ancestors. The Celts saw this phase as a space between worlds, a time conducive to divination practices, such as reading runes and black mirrors, and for rituals of spiritual healing and self-knowledge. On Black Moon nights, it was common for druids and sages to isolate themselves to meditate and receive visions, using herbs such as mugwort to facilitate altered states of consciousness. In addition, this was the ideal time to renew spiritual vows and prepare for the rebirth of the New Moon, ending a cycle with wisdom and keen intuition.

By working with these lunar phases, the Celts not only strengthened their magic, but also learned to flow with the natural rhythms of life. The Moon was more than a celestial body; it was a guide, a silent teacher that taught about the right time to plant, grow, harvest, and rest. By rescuing this knowledge today, we can reconnect with our essence, understand that we are part of a greater flow, and use lunar magic as a powerful tool for transformation, balance, and self-discovery.

The Moon continues to remind us that life is made of cycles, of beginnings and endings, of moments of expansion and retreat. Just as the ancient Celts found in the Moon an ally for their magic and spirituality, we can also tune in to its phases to better understand our own internal rhythms. By observing its light and feeling its influence, we realize that there is a right time for everything, and that trusting this natural flow allows us to walk with more wisdom and harmony. Whether to manifest dreams, release what no longer serves us, or simply contemplate its silvery beauty in the sky, the Moon remains a beacon, guiding us in the eternal dance of life.

Chapter 28
Spells and Enchantments

In Celtic tradition, magic was an intertwining of words, intention, and the forces of nature, reflecting the belief that everything in the universe was alive and pulsed with sacred energy. Spells and enchantments were more than mere mystical formulas; they represented the ability to manipulate reality by connecting with the elements, the gods, and ancestral spirits. For the Celts, every sound emitted carried vibrational power, and words spoken with intention and knowledge could shape events, attract blessings, and ward off danger. The use of verbal magic was a secret mastered primarily by the Druids, who held the knowledge of sacred languages and rhythmic combinations capable of enhancing spells. However, this wisdom also permeated the daily lives of the Celtic people, who used simple enchantments for protection, healing, and prosperity.

The structure of Celtic spells was based on principles that ensured their effectiveness and alignment with natural energies. Before casting a spell, it was essential that the practitioner be in tune with their intention, as clarity of purpose determined the direction of the channeled energy. Concentration was another indispensable element, allowing the mind to remain focused and free from distractions. Additionally, visualization was a common practice, in which the desired outcome was imagined as if it had already materialized, strengthening magical manifestation. Words of power, often passed down through generations, were carefully chosen, as the Celts believed that certain sounds and phonetic combinations possessed a special magnetism to invoke spiritual forces. Along with words, the use of natural elements—such as herbs, stones, candles, and sacred symbols—helped channel the energy needed for each spell. In this way, Celtic magic was not limited to a mere act of manipulation, but was a harmonious interaction with the flow of the universe, respecting the cycles of nature and spiritual laws.

Each spell was molded according to its purpose and could be performed simply or in elaborate rituals, depending on the need and experience of the practitioner. Healing spells were widely used, taking advantage of the properties of herbs and sacred words to restore balance to body and spirit. Protective enchantments created barriers against harmful energies, either through the creation of amulets or the recitation of magic verses in times of danger. To attract prosperity, the Celts resorted to formulas that combined elements such as coins, grains, and symbolic gestures, reinforcing the intention of abundance. Love spells, in turn, focused on harmony and the attraction of genuine connections, never forcing wills, but rather opening paths for encounters aligned with destiny. Regardless of intention, each spell was performed with respect, gratitude, and awareness of the responsibility involved in magical practice. Even today, Celtic verbal magic teaches us that words are more than mere expressions: they are creative forces capable of shaping our reality, connecting us to the sacred, and awakening the power that resides within us.

The Druids, guardians of ancestral wisdom, were masters in the art of spells and enchantments, deeply knowledgeable about the power of words and the secrets of verbal magic. Their ability to manipulate the energy of the universe through sacred language made them revered figures within Celtic society, responsible for mediating contact with the gods, protecting the community, and ensuring harmony between the visible and invisible worlds. They developed intricate magical formulas, combining carefully chosen words with melodic rhythms, powerful rhymes, and evocative imagery. This knowledge was passed down orally from generation to generation, preserving the tradition and effectiveness of enchantments. Each word uttered had a specific purpose, and its intonation and cadence were as important as its meaning. The sound of the voice, combined with intention and ritual gestures, created a flow of energy that connected to the forces of nature, manifesting changes in reality.

Spells and enchantments had various applications in the lives of the Celts. They were used for the healing of diseases, mobilizing the properties of sacred herbs and spiritual energy to restore the balance of body and soul. They were also used as protection against evil forces and misfortunes, erecting magical barriers around individuals or communities. To ensure good harvests and abundance, the Druids cast enchantments on the fields, blessing the land and invoking the generosity of the gods. In the emotional field, love spells were not aimed at manipulation or imposing feelings, but rather at opening paths and attracting connections aligned with the destiny of those involved. Each enchantment was performed with deep respect for the laws of the universe, as it was believed that magic, when used irresponsibly or selfishly, would return to the conjurer with equal intensity.

For a Celtic spell to be effective, it needed to contain some fundamental elements. The first of these was intention, considered the heart of magic. Before starting any enchantment, the practitioner should be fully aware of what they wanted to achieve, formulating their intention with precision and charging it with emotion. The strength of desire and belief in fulfillment were indispensable for the energy to move correctly. Next, concentration played a crucial role, as scattering thoughts or doubting one's own power could weaken the magic. During the spell, the practitioner should keep their mind free from distractions and focused exclusively on the desired purpose.

Visualization was another essential element. The Celts believed that by vividly imagining the outcome as if it had already materialized, the practitioner strengthened the manifestation of their will. Thus, when casting a healing spell, for example, one should visualize the person already healthy and full of vitality, feeling the joy of recovery. This practice intensified the connection between the physical and spiritual world, allowing energy to flow more easily towards the realization of desire.

Furthermore, words of power played a central role in spells. Enchantments could be intoned in the Celtic language, an ancestral dialect, or even a personal language, as long as they carried the necessary intention and were pronounced with conviction. Some terms and expressions were considered especially sacred, and when repeated in a certain cadence or in conjunction with ritual gestures, they became even more potent. Many of these words of power were passed down from master to apprentice, ensuring that the magical tradition remained alive.

Magical elements were also fundamental to enhance a spell. Sacred herbs, crystals, candles, incense, and specific symbols were chosen according to the nature of the enchantment. Herbs carried spiritual properties that aided in the manifestation of intention; crystals served as conductors of energy; candles represented the fire of transformation; incense purified the environment and strengthened the connection with spirits; and sacred symbols, drawn in the air or on objects, sealed the energy of the spell. Each element was carefully integrated into the ritual, strengthening the link between the practitioner and natural forces.

The ritual, in turn, was the structure that unified all these elements. Created to concentrate energy, it involved gestures, movements, and symbolic actions that amplified the power of the enchantment. From lighting a candle and drawing sigils to chanting songs and walking magic circles, each act within the ritual had a purpose and contributed to the effectiveness of the spell. The repetition of these gestures reinforced the intention and created a link with the spiritual energies that would assist in the manifestation of desire.

Among the best known Celtic spells, those of healing, protection, and love stood out. The healing spell, for example, required the use of healing herbs such as chamomile, lavender, and rosemary, combined with restorative energy crystals, such as clear quartz and amethyst. The practitioner would light a green candle, a symbol of renewal and life, and visualize the sick person being enveloped by a healing light. With the recitation of an enchantment, the gods and spirits of nature were asked to restore the individual's health. This spell not only accelerated recovery, but also strengthened the spirit and balanced emotions.

The protection spell, on the other hand, was widely used to ward off negative energies and create a barrier against harmful influences. For this, herbs such as rosemary, rue, and laurel were burned or scattered around the environment, while crystals such as black tourmaline and obsidian were strategically positioned around the space or carried as amulets. A white candle, representing the protective light, was lit and a shield of energy was visualized forming around the individual. The enchantment uttered sealed this protection, ensuring spiritual and emotional security.

The love spell, in turn, was performed to attract genuine connections and strengthen emotional bonds.

Herbs such as rose, jasmine, and verbena were combined with crystals such as rose quartz and moonstone, amplifying the energy of love and harmony. The pink candle, a symbol of passion and sincere affection, was lit while the practitioner visualized the loved one approaching, enveloped by an aura of affection and complicity. The enchantment, sung with sweetness and faith, served to open paths to true love, always respecting free will and the will of those involved.

Celtic spells and enchantments are a powerful tool for connecting with the universe, allowing the practitioner's will to manifest in alignment with natural energies. More than mere magic formulas, they represent the harmonious interaction between the human being and spiritual forces, teaching that true power resides in intention, wisdom, and respect for the laws of the cosmos. By using verbal magic with awareness and devotion, we awaken our inner strength and shape our reality in a balanced and sacred way.

The practice of Celtic spells and enchantments reminds us that true magic is not only in the rituals or elements used, but in the intention we put into each word and action. By connecting with this ancient tradition, we learn that magic is a reflection of the harmony between our desire, our energy, and the natural flow of the universe. Thus, when we pronounce an enchantment or perform a ritual, we are not only manipulating invisible forces, but reaffirming our personal power and our connection to the sacred. In the end, magic is, above all, an act of awareness and respect, a dance between the visible and the invisible, in which each of us is both the sorcerer and the enchantment.

Chapter 29
Talismans and Amulets

In the Celtic universe, where magic and spirituality are inseparably intertwined, objects were not mere ornaments or utilities, but extensions of the very essence of the invisible world. Each piece carried with it the strength of ancestral traditions, conveying deep meanings that went beyond mere aesthetics or material value. Talismans and amulets emerged as fundamental elements in everyday life, imbued with power and symbolism, serving both as protectors against adverse forces and as channelers of blessings and good energies. The Celts' relationship with these objects went beyond physical possession; it was a sacred bond between the individual, the spirits of nature, and the divine forces that governed the cosmos. Created with carefully chosen materials and consecrated by specific rituals, these artifacts were testimonies to the unwavering belief in the interaction between the tangible and the spiritual, shaping the way the Celts understood and influenced their own destiny.

The Celtic worldview was strongly grounded in the interconnectedness of all things, and talismans and amulets represented this continuous link between the human being and the universe. They were not only used to attract fortune or ward off evil, but also to strengthen the bond between the community and natural energies, conferring protection, courage, wisdom, and even promoting health. Stones, metals, wood, bones, shells, and other natural elements were selected according to their vibration and spiritual significance. The act of wearing or gifting an amulet carried with it the intention of nurturing this invisible bond and ensuring that the forces of nature were in harmony with the wearer. Over the centuries, this practice has not only endured but evolved, keeping its essence alive within modern cultures that still seek in Celtic ancestry a path to balance and energetic protection.

The sacred character of talismans and amulets was also reflected in the way they were made and consecrated. The artisan, when carving, molding, or engraving a symbol, not only created an object, but impregnated it with their intention and devotion, making it a channel of personal and spiritual power. Each piece was unique, as the energy applied during its creation differentiated it from the others, ensuring that it served the specific purpose for which it was intended. In this way, these artifacts became true magical allies, reinforcing the Celtic belief that the interaction between the visible and the invisible not only existed, but could be consciously manipulated for personal and collective benefit.

The Celts deeply believed that certain objects, whether found in nature or meticulously crafted by man, possessed inherent magical properties. Raw stones, shimmering crystals, animal bones fallen in natural rituals, shells brought in by the tides, wood sculpted by time, and metals molded by fire were carefully chosen and transformed into powerful talismans and amulets. Each element carried with it not only its physical composition, but also its spiritual vibration and its meaning within the complex Celtic belief system. The process of creating these sacred objects was full of intention, respect, and connection with the invisible forces of the world, ensuring that they became true extensions of the will of those who wore them.

Talismans, in turn, were created with a clear and positive purpose: to attract what was desired, be it luck, prosperity, love, or abundance. They were made with symbolic elements that represented fertility, wealth, and growth. Images of animals and plants, which carried mystical meanings, were often carved in stone or wood. Protective gods were engraved in metal, becoming powerful intermediaries between the spiritual and earthly worlds. Coins and precious stones, with their natural vibrations of prosperity, were used to amplify the magnetism of the talisman. More than mere objects, these artifacts were energy channelers, charged with the intention of the one who created and used them. For a talisman to work effectively, it was believed that it was necessary to consecrate it in a ritual, where the will of the wearer united with the forces of nature, sealing the purpose of the object in the fabric of the universe.

Amulets, on the other hand, had a different function, aimed at protection and creating a shield against negative energies and unwanted influences. While talismans attracted blessings, amulets warded off danger. Many were engraved with sacred symbols, such as the Celtic knot, whose intertwined shape represented the eternal interconnection of all things and the strength of spiritual protection. The Celtic cross, combining the solar wheel with the traditional cross, was a powerful emblem of faith and hope, invoking the presence of the divine for the defense of the bearer. The triskele, with its three spirals in motion, symbolized the harmony between the three Celtic worlds - earth, sea, and sky - and was often used to maintain balance and ward off disruptive forces. In addition to symbols, amulets could also incorporate natural elements of strong protective power. Herbs such as rosemary and rue were dried and carried in small bags, forming living amulets that exuded their protective energy. Crystals such as black tourmaline and obsidian were used to absorb and dissipate negative energies, creating a field of defense around those who carried them.

The creation of these artifacts was a deeply spiritual and respectful practice, requiring more than manual skill: it required connection with natural forces and with the gods. The process began with the selection of materials, which were never harvested carelessly. If a stone was removed from the earth, thanks were given to nature. If a wood was chosen, permission was asked from the spirit of the tree. This act of respect ensured that the object would carry good energies and fulfill its purpose effectively. During the making, the craftsman kept his mind focused on the intention of the object, infusing it with his personal energy. Each chisel blow, each carved line, each woven thread was an act of magic, transforming a simple item into a powerful channel of invisible forces.

The use of talismans and amulets was varied, adapting to individual and collective needs. Many were worn as jewelry - pendants, necklaces, bracelets, rings, and brooches - to ensure that they were always in contact with the body, emanating their influence on the wearer. Others were kept at home or in the workplace, protecting the environment from negative energies and attracting good vibes to the space. On altars dedicated to gods and ancestors, amulets and talismans were arranged as offerings and tools of spiritual connection, amplifying the energy of rituals and strengthening the link between worlds. In moments of great importance, such as battles, harvests, or union ceremonies, these objects were used to ensure success and protection, reinforcing the belief that destiny could be shaped by interaction with the sacred.

The symbolism present in these artifacts was what gave them power. The Celts attributed deep meanings to various symbols, understanding that each of them carried a unique and specific vibration. The Celtic knot represented not only protection, but also the interconnection of life and eternity, being one of the most common in protective amulets. The Celtic cross symbolized the union of the physical and spiritual worlds, being used to ensure balance and strength. The triskele evoked the constant movement of life, renewal, and the energy of the three natural realms, making it a symbol of transformation and progress. The spiral, which appeared on many ancient stones, represented growth, evolution, and connection to the cosmos, being a powerful emblem of personal development. In addition, animals also played a significant role within Celtic magical symbolism. The bear was associated with strength and courage, the boar with fertility and abundance, the raven with wisdom and mystery, and the salmon with knowledge and persistence.

By understanding the depth of the Celts' relationship with their talismans and amulets, we can see a people whose spirituality permeated every aspect of daily life. These objects were not mere adornments or empty superstitions, but tangible expressions of a worldview in which the sacred and the mundane intertwined inseparably. Today, inspired by this ancestral tradition, we can create our own talismans and amulets, charging them with our purest intentions and using them as tools to establish a deeper connection with the energy of the universe. Whether to attract luck, protect against adversity, or seek balance, these artifacts continue to carry the wisdom of the ancient Celts, guiding those who seek to live in harmony with the invisible forces that govern existence.

More than mere objects, talismans and amulets were testimonies to the Celts' deep connection to the sacred, symbols of a faith that permeated every aspect of life. By carrying them, they not only sought protection or luck, but reaffirmed their communion with the forces of nature and the mysteries of the universe. Today, as we reclaim this ancestral knowledge, we learn that true magic is not in the object itself, but in the intention and energy we place in it. Thus, when we choose or create our own amulets, we continue a millennial tradition, keeping alive the wisdom of the ancients and strengthening our own spiritual journey.

Chapter 30
The Way of the Warrior

In Celtic society, the warrior was more than just a fighter; he personified the protective force of the community, a symbol of honor, courage and spiritual connection. His role transcended the art of war and intertwined with philosophy, leadership and devotion to the sacred. For the Celts, battle was not just a physical confrontation, but a manifestation of the harmony between body, mind and spirit. The true warrior was not the one who wielded the sword with brutality, but the one who understood the need for balance, respect for traditions and unwavering commitment to his people. From youth, he was prepared not only for fighting, but for life, being trained in strategies, diplomatic skills and moral values that would guide his path. This journey was not limited to rigorous physical training, but also a quest for self-knowledge, discipline and communion with cosmic forces.

The Celts did not glorify war for violence, but for the defense of what was right and sacred. Battle was seen as a last resort, a means of protecting the land, culture and honor of the clan. The warrior was a guardian, not a conqueror. His sword, shield and spear were not just instruments of combat, but extensions of his own essence, carrying his determination and loyalty. At the same time, his connection to the gods and ancestors gave him a greater sense of purpose, making war an act not only of strength, but of spiritual significance. The rites of passage, the solemn oaths and the symbols they carried on their bodies and weapons reinforced this sacred bond, constantly reminding them that their struggle was also a way of honoring their lineage and the spirits that guided them.

More than a protector of his people, the Celtic warrior was a seeker of truth and wisdom. He understood that the greatest battle did not take place only on the battlefield, but within himself. Overcoming fear, mastering one's own impulses and acting justly were challenges as great as any physical confrontation. The warrior's journey was, above all, an inner journey. He sought not only victory over his enemies, but the perfecting of his spirit and the building of a legacy of honor. Inspired by these principles, the Celts teach us that true power lies not only in the strength of arms, but in the righteousness of the heart and the wisdom of every choice made throughout life.

For the Celts, war was an inescapable reality, but never an end in itself. The Celtic warrior did not surrender to battle out of mere desire for conquest or pleasure in violence, but out of a duty to protect his people, his land and his ancestral values. More than a fighter, he was a guardian, someone who carried with him the sacred commitment to preserve harmony and justice. His courage, honor and loyalty were not limited to the battlefield, but permeated every aspect of his life.

For him, strength could not exist without compassion, and power without balance. It was within this deep understanding that the warrior's code of conduct developed, a set of values and principles that guided his journey and shaped his character.

From a very young age, the aspiring warrior began his training, an arduous process that involved not only physical improvement, but also intellectual and spiritual development. Resistance and dexterity were cultivated through constant exercises that strengthened the body, preparing it for the challenges of combat. The handling of the sword, spear and shield was taught with precision, as was the use of the bow and dagger. However, war was not won only by the strength of arms, and young warriors were equally trained in the art of strategy, diplomacy and leadership. Understanding the enemy's movements, anticipating their actions and knowing when to attack or retreat was as important as wielding a weapon skillfully. In addition, they learned the importance of discipline, courage and loyalty, being encouraged to always act with respect and righteousness. A warrior could not be guided by impulse or anger; each blow struck should have a purpose, each decision made should be in harmony with the values of the clan.

The code of honor of the Celtic warriors was unbreakable. They fought not only for themselves, but for the greater good of their community, committing themselves to defending the weakest and facing any threat that endangered the safety of their people. Justice was a fundamental pillar of this code, and truth a sacred duty. Lies and betrayals were seen as serious affronts, capable of forever tarnishing a warrior's reputation. Cowardice was not tolerated, as a true fighter should face challenges head-on, without hesitation or fear. Honor lay not only in victory, but in the way one conducted oneself in all situations. The given word had an inestimable weight, and breaking an oath meant losing dignity and the respect of one's peers. Therefore, each warrior was taught to carefully measure his promises, for once made, they should be kept at all costs.

Spirituality also played a central role in the life of the Celtic warrior. He did not see his strength as an isolated attribute, but as an extension of something much greater - a deep connection to the gods, ancestral spirits and the forces of nature. Before battles, rituals were performed to ask for divine protection and guidance, and many warriors carried talismans and sacred symbols to strengthen their spirits in combat. It was believed that a warrior's bravery and luck were directly linked to his relationship with the spiritual world. For them, each battle was not just an earthly dispute, but a reflection of cosmic forces in action. And so, with reverence, the warriors honored not only their gods, but also those who came before them, for they knew that their deeds would be remembered by the descendants who would come after.

More than just a defender of his people, the Celtic warrior was an essential pillar of the community. His role went beyond battles and armed confrontations. He was a leader, an example of courage and wisdom, someone who inspired respect and admiration. When not at war, many warriors devoted themselves to protecting the villagers, resolving internal disputes and advising the younger ones. His presence conveyed security, and his word often carried weight equivalent to that of the druids and elders. His commitment to the well-being of the people did not end when he put away his sword, for he understood that true strength lay in the unity and prosperity of the community.

But the greatest battle a Celtic warrior faced was not waged against external enemies, but within himself. He understood that mastering his own fears, passions and impulses was as arduous a challenge as any physical combat. The search for truth and justice was a constant path, and each decision made shaped not only his trajectory, but also his legacy. The Celtic warrior did not fight just to win; he fought to become better, to evolve as a human being and to find the balance between strength and compassion. His journey was not just a destination, but a continuous process of growth and transformation.

As we reflect on the path of the Celtic warrior, we can see that his wisdom transcends time and continues to echo in our reality. His values teach us that true strength lies not only in the ability to fight, but in the ability to remain true to our principles, even in the face of adversity. His code of honor reminds us of the importance of truth, loyalty and respect. And his connection to the sacred shows us that to be truly powerful, we need to be in harmony with ourselves and the world around us. Thus, by drawing inspiration from these ancient warriors, we can find within ourselves the courage to face our own challenges and the determination to move forward with honor and purpose.

The path of the Celtic warrior was not traveled only with weapons and battles, but with the courage to face oneself, the commitment to truth and the incessant search for balance between strength and compassion. His legacy transcends time, teaching that true victory lies not only in external conquest, but in the honor of living according to high principles. Today, as we look at this journey, we realize that all of us, in some way, carry the spirit of the warrior within us - ready to fight for what is right, to surpass ourselves every day and to write our own story with dignity and purpose.

Chapter 31
The Way of the Artisan

In Celtic tradition, the artisan was not just a skilled creator of objects, but a true intermediary between the earthly and spiritual worlds, someone capable of translating into matter the essence of the invisible forces that governed existence. His craft was not limited to technique, but involved a deep connection with the natural elements, with the cycles of life and with the sacred energy that permeated all things. Each piece produced was more than just a utensil or ornament; it was a reflection of the creator's soul, a channel of cultural and spiritual expression, laden with symbolism and intention. Celtic craftsmanship was not just a functional practice, but a living art that preserved stories, honored the gods and strengthened the bonds between generations. Creating an object, for a Celtic artisan, was an act of devotion and respect, where the choice of materials, the shape and the details were guided both by ancestral knowledge and by the inspiration granted by the gods.

The artisan's connection to nature was sacred and inseparable. The wood extracted from revered trees, the metal molded with dexterity and the clay worked with patience were not just raw materials, but living entities, endowed with their own energy. Before harvesting any resource, the Celtic craftsman performed rituals of thanksgiving, asking permission from the earth and recognizing the spirit contained in each element. This respect for nature ensured that the creative process was a balanced exchange, where the raw material was given new life in the form of art, keeping its spiritual essence intact. Thus, a carved amulet, a forged jewel or a painted ceramic piece were not just products of manual skill, but containers of power, capable of transmitting protection, wisdom and strength to those who possessed them.

More than just a craft, Celtic craftsmanship was a bridge between the past and the present, carrying with it the myths, beliefs and values of a people deeply connected to the sacred. The intertwined patterns, the engraved symbols and the techniques passed down from master to apprentice ensured that the Celtic cultural identity remained alive, even in the face of the changes and challenges of time. Even today, this legacy continues to inspire artists and creators around the world, reminding us that true art lies not only in the beauty of form, but in the intention and soul that are imprinted in every detail. The path of the Celtic artisan teaches us that creativity, when combined with respect for tradition and spirituality, becomes a powerful force for transformation, capable of connecting the human being to the divine and giving life to objects that tell stories beyond words.

The Celtic artisan worked with natural materials, extracted from the earth with reverence and gratitude. Wood, metal, stone, vegetable fibers and leather were his main raw materials, and each had its own energy, a spirit that needed to be respected and honored. Before harvesting the wood, the craftsman prayed to the spirit of the tree, asking permission to remove a branch or a fallen trunk. The metal was extracted and molded with a deep sense of sacredness, as the Celts believed that minerals came from the bowels of the earth, the womb of the Great Mother, and therefore should be worked with respect. The clay, molded by hands and fire, carried the essence of the four elements: earth, water, air and fire. Each piece created was unique, not only because of the craftsman's skill, but because it carried within itself the fusion between the creator's energy, the inspiration of nature and the blessing of the gods.

More than just a craft, Celtic craftsmanship was a manifestation of the soul of the people, a reflection of their spirituality and their connection to the natural and invisible world. Each object produced contained a purpose, whether practical, decorative or ritualistic. A richly adorned bronze brooch was not just an ornament, but also a protective amulet; a knife worked with symbolic details was more than a tool - it was a sacred instrument, used in rites and ceremonies. The act of creating was seen not only as work, but as a dialogue with the forces of nature and with the ancestors who, through the hands of the craftsman, transmitted their knowledge and blessings.

The Celtic craftsman lived according to fundamental values that guided his practice and gave meaning to his art. The first of these was absolute respect for nature, the source of all raw material and all inspiration. The craftsman's relationship with the land was not one of exploitation, but of partnership. Each resource harvested was used consciously, ensuring that nothing was wasted and that the harmony of natural cycles was preserved. In addition, there was an unwavering commitment to excellence. Learning to master materials and techniques was a long and arduous path, and the craftsman dedicated years to improving his skills. From a young age, he learned from a master and practiced tirelessly until he reached a level of mastery worthy of the gods.

Creativity also played an essential role in the work of the Celtic craftsman. Inspired by the forms of nature, myths and visions transmitted through dreams and meditation, he constantly sought to innovate and create pieces that were not only beautiful, but full of meaning. Originality was a valued gift, as it was believed that art was a divine gift. To create was a sacred act, and for this reason, the craftsman often performed rituals before starting a new work. He could light candles, offer herbs to the spirits of the earth or chant songs to invoke the inspiration of the gods.

Each piece created was imbued with magic and spirituality. The Celts believed that certain symbols and enchantments could confer protection, strength or wisdom to objects. Therefore, it was common for the craftsman to engrave spirals, Celtic knots and representations of animals in his works, loading them with meaning. In addition to visible symbols, many objects possessed hidden blessings. A craftsman could whisper words of power over a jewel while polishing it, or bury a piece of metal in the earth for a night to absorb the energy of nature before it was finished. This ritualistic aspect of craftsmanship ensured that objects were not only functional, but also vehicles of spiritual power.

Celtic craftsmanship was not just a means of survival, but a way of preserving culture, transmitting stories and reinforcing the identity of the people. Each piece carried within itself the myths and values of the Celts, perpetuating their tradition from generation to generation. Through the work of artisans, sacred symbols were kept alive, and the beliefs of the people continued to be honored. Thus, craftsmanship became a link between the past and the present, a testimony to ancestral wisdom and a guide for those who came after.

Among the main forms of crafts practiced by the Celts, metallurgy occupied a prominent place. Masters in the art of working bronze, iron and gold, the Celts created weapons, tools, jewelry and ceremonial objects of impressive beauty and complexity. Metalworking was associated with the god Lugh, lord of skill and knowledge. A Celtic blacksmith was not just a craftsman, but a guardian of ancient secrets, an alchemist who mastered fire and the transformation of elements.

Pottery was also widely practiced, producing vases, bowls and other ceramic containers used both in everyday life and in rituals. This art was linked to the goddess Brigid, patroness of poetry, healing and the arts. The act of shaping clay was seen as a reflection of the very cycle of life, where raw material was transformed by fire to acquire shape and resistance.

Woodworking, in turn, was a fundamental skill. The Celts were skilled carpenters and carvers, creating furniture, sculptures, household utensils and ritual objects. The wood of sacred trees, such as oak and yew, was especially valued. Often, a simple staff or a carved wooden amulet was more than just an object - it was a channel of connection with the spirits of the forest.

Basketry and the weaving of vegetable fibers were another important aspect of Celtic craftsmanship. With refined techniques, the Celts produced baskets, mats and even resistant clothing. These works were linked to the cycles of nature and the very structure of life, reflecting the idea that everything was interconnected.

Celtic jewelry, in turn, was true works of art. Made of gold, silver and bronze, they were adorned with precious stones, enamels and complex intertwined designs. More than just adornments, these jewels carried deep spiritual and social significance. Some rings and brooches were passed down from generation to generation as symbols of lineage and protection.

The legacy of the Celtic craftsman survives to this day. His worldview, his dedication to art and his respect for nature continue to inspire artists and creators around the world. In a time when mass production dominates the market, Celtic craftsmanship reminds us of the value of manual labor, the connection between the creator and his creation and the importance of preserving history and spirituality through art. By understanding this tradition, we can find inspiration to develop our own skills, cultivate respect for nature and rediscover the transformative power of creativity. After all, art, when done with soul, is able to transcend time and tell stories that echo beyond words.

    Celtic craftsmanship remains a living testament to the soul of a people who knew how to transform matter into memory, devotion into form and spirituality into art. Each piece created was more than a reflection of skill; it was a portal between worlds, a legacy printed on wood, metal or stone that has withstood time and continues to inspire. Even today, when we admire a Celtic knot, an ancestral brooch or a sculpture laden with symbolism, we are reminded that true art lies not only in the beauty of the work, but in the story it carries and the energy that pulsates in each line carved by the hands of the creator.

Chapter 32
The Path of the Bard

In Celtic tradition, the figure of the bard was revered as a living link between the past and the present, a guardian of collective memory, and a transmitter of ancestral wisdom. Their gift transcended the ability to compose verses or play melodies; they were masters of word and music, whose voices resonated in the hearts of their people like an invisible thread connecting them to the essence of their culture. Their art was not limited to aesthetics but had a sacred purpose: to record the deeds of heroes, preserve genealogies, narrate myths and legends, and keep alive the lessons that guided the community's path. In a world where orality was the main form of perpetuating knowledge, the bard played a fundamental role, ensuring that the stories of their people were never lost in time.

The path of the bard was not only an artistic journey but also a spiritual one. Every word uttered carried immense weight, for the Celts believed that speech possessed a magical power capable of influencing reality. The bard mastered this force, using it to inspire, instruct, and even transform destinies. Their apprenticeship began early, requiring years of dedication to memorize entire epics, understand the symbols and metaphors of tradition, and perfect their ability to move and persuade. In addition to poetry and music, they also mastered rhetoric, diplomacy, and the ability to create subtle metaphors to convey profound truths. The respect and influence they held in Celtic society reflected their importance: kings and leaders often consulted them to make decisions and seek guidance.

More than a storyteller, the bard was a guardian of the sacred. Their songs not only narrated the past but also connected listeners to the spiritual world. They knew how to evoke the forces of nature, how to use rhythm and melody to heal, and how to channel messages from the gods and ancestors. Their role was to unite, inspire, and strengthen the spirit of the community, ensuring that the essential truths of their culture were never dissipated. Even today, the legacy of the bard survives in those who use words and music to touch souls, connect stories, and keep alive the roots of their identity.

The path of the Celtic bard was a journey of deep connection with words, music, history, and spirituality. From childhood, bards were initiated into the art of poetry, music, storytelling, and rhetoric, undergoing rigorous training that prepared them to be not only artists but also guardians of the collective memory of their people. Their learning went far beyond technique; it required an immersion in the mysteries of the oral tradition and the magic of the word, for speech was not just a means of communication but a creative force capable of shaping reality.

At the heart of Celtic tradition, the bard was much more than a mere singer or poet; they were a historian and genealogist, charged with preserving the memory of their people. Through their songs and narratives, they recorded heroic deeds, epic battles, myths, and legends, ensuring that the cultural identity of the community remained intact across generations. Each name, each event, and each lineage were immortalized in carefully composed verses, passed down from master to apprentice with the precision of one who knew that the history of the people depended on their fidelity to detail.

But their art was not restricted to history. As a poet and musician, the bard possessed the gift of touching the heart and soul through the harmony of words and the melody of instruments. Their compositions were not just for entertainment; they expressed deep emotions, celebrated life, honored the gods, and strengthened the community's bonds with the sacred. With their harp, flute, or drum, they could both lull a child to sleep and inspire warriors before a battle, for each note carried meaning, each sound a bridge between the human and the divine.

The bard was also, above all, a master storyteller. Their talent went beyond words; they knew how to use their voice, body, and expression to transport their audience to other worlds and other times. Their narratives were not just accounts of the past but portals to the imagination, evoking vivid images and intense emotions that captivated everyone's attention. Their gift of persuasion was so powerful that they could transform a simple story into a life lesson, awakening deep reflections in those who listened.

Furthermore, the bard played an essential role as guardian of the oral tradition. In a culture where writing was not the primary means of preserving knowledge, it was up to them to ensure that ancestral teachings, values, and customs were passed down through generations. Their voices carried the wisdom of the ancients, their music echoed the essential truths of their people, and their responsibility was immense, for without them, the collective memory could be lost over time.

For this reason, bards were also seen as intermediaries between worlds. Their sensitivity allowed them to connect with the gods, ancestors, and forces of nature, acting as channels between the visible and the invisible. Often, their compositions were inspired by dreams, visions, or signs from nature, and their words could carry messages from beyond. When they chanted their songs in rituals and ceremonies, it was believed that they were able to invoke powerful energies, bring blessings, or even alter the course of events.

The Celts had a deep belief in the power of the spoken and sung word. For them, language was an active force in the universe, capable of influencing reality, manifesting desires, and evoking the energies of the cosmos. A skilled bard mastered this art with expertise, knowing how to choose each word to create specific effects, whether to inspire courage, awaken love, or even cast curses. Their voice could raise kings or bring down tyrants, for their influence went beyond mere speech: it resonated in the soul of their people.

Music, in turn, was also considered a form of magic. Bards knew that certain melodies had the power to heal wounds, soothe sorrows, strengthen spirits, and protect against negative influences. It was not uncommon for a bard to be called upon to play at important moments, such as births, weddings, battles, and funerals, as their presence brought balance and harmony to the environment. Their songs, permeated with hidden meanings and vibrating in tune with the universe, created a sacred atmosphere that connected listeners to the spiritual world.

In Celtic society, bards occupied a prestigious position, being respected not only for their art but also for their wisdom and connection to the sacred. They were not just itinerant artists, but advisors to kings, judges, diplomats, and teachers. Their voices could be used to pacify conflicts, inspire leaders, and even influence political decisions. In a time when words had sacred weight, bards were the holders of the greatest power of all: the power to shape thoughts, inspire hearts, and keep alive the essence of a people.

This legacy survives to this day, inspiring musicians, writers, poets, and spiritual seekers around the world. The art of the Celtic bard, laden with beauty, magic, and meaning, continues to echo in modern times, reminding us of the importance of honoring the word, preserving our stories, and using music as a bridge to the sacred. In a world increasingly lacking connection with its roots, the example of the bards teaches us to value our own voice, our own melody, and to find our own way of telling the story that dwells within our soul.

The legacy of the bard transcends time, resonating with those who still find in words and melody a path to truth and connection with the sacred. Each story told, each song sung, continues to echo like an invisible thread between the past and the present, uniting generations through art and memory. As long as there are voices willing to sing, narrate, and inspire, the spirit of the bard will never be silenced, and their mission to preserve the essence of a people will remain alive, guiding those who seek meaning in the magic of words.

Chapter 33
Living Celtic Spirituality

Celtic spirituality invites you on a journey of deep connection with nature, with the sacred, and with the very essence of being. Unlike dogmatic traditions, its path is fluid, intuitive, and deeply rooted in the observation of the natural world and the cycles of life. Living this spirituality does not require temples or rigid rituals, but rather an awakening of perception to the subtle signs of the earth, wind, waters, and fire. Each season, each change in the landscape, each creature that inhabits the forests and rivers carries a message, and it is up to the practitioner to develop the sensitivity to understand it. Integrating this vision into everyday life is to cultivate a harmonious existence, where every action, every thought, and every intention resonates with the ancestral wisdom of the Celts, transforming the ordinary into the sacred.

This journey begins by recognizing that Celtic spirituality does not separate the divine from the material world but sees it pulsating in every tree, in every stone, and in the very flow of life. Observing the movement of the seasons, feeling the energy of the elements, and perceiving the subtle dance between birth, growth, decline, and rebirth allows one to align with the rhythm of the universe. Celebrating seasonal festivals, such as Samhain, Beltane, and Lughnasadh, is not just about honoring tradition, but about synchronizing with the primordial forces that sustain existence. Small daily gestures, such as walking in nature with awareness, lighting a candle in honor of ancestors, or simply being silent to hear the voice of the wind, are ways of living this connection.

In addition to observation and attunement to nature, living Celtic spirituality means acting with integrity, honor, and respect for the cycles and relationships that weave the great flow of life. Intuition is valued as a powerful guide, and the practice of magic - understood as the manifestation of will aligned with the universe - can manifest itself in various ways: from the use of herbs and amulets to the power of words and music to transform reality. The Celtic path is not just a set of beliefs, but a state of being, where each gesture carries intention, each word has power, and each moment can be a doorway to the sacred. By awakening this awareness, life becomes a flow of magic and meaning, where the ordinary and the divine meet in perfect harmony.

To live Celtic spirituality on a daily basis, it is essential to create moments of genuine connection with nature, which is seen as a sacred temple. More than just contact, this interaction must be intentional and profound. Walking through a forest or park can become an act of contemplation, where each leaf, each breeze, and each bird song brings a message. Sitting under a tree is not just resting, but feeling its energy, connecting with its deep roots, and absorbing the silent wisdom it holds. Watching the sunrise ceases to be a commonplace habit and becomes a ritual of renewal, an invitation to tune in to the cycles of light and shadow. Cultivating a garden becomes more than a hobby, but an act of co-creation with the earth, a link with the forces of growth and renewal. This constant interaction with the elements allows one to feel the presence of the sacred in every aspect of the natural world, strengthening the bond between the human being and the spirit of the earth.

The Celts honored the cycles of life as reflections of universal rhythms. Just as nature goes through phases of growth, fullness, decline, and renewal, each person also goes through their own inner seasons. Celebrating the seasonal festivals of the Wheel of the Year is not just about reliving a tradition, but about realigning with these primordial forces. Samhain marks the end and the beginning, a time for introspection and honoring ancestors. Beltane celebrates life and fertility, bringing joy and passion to the spirit. Lughnasadh is a time of harvest, gratitude, and recognition for the fruits of labor and dedication. Observing the changes in the seasons and reflecting on the personal transformations that happen in parallel strengthens this connection. Honoring one's own cycles means accepting that each phase of life has its beauty and purpose - moments of growth and learning, periods of withdrawal and healing, phases of expansion and celebration.

Gratitude is a fundamental pillar of this spirituality. Recognizing and giving thanks for the blessings received expands the connection with the natural flow of abundance. This feeling need not be reserved for major events; on the contrary, it should permeate everyday life, valuing everything from food on the table to the presence of loved ones. A simple gesture, such as lighting a candle at dusk and thanking the gods and ancestors for protection, can transform the energy of an environment. Creating a gratitude journal, writing down something you feel blessed for every day, strengthens this practice and brings a more attentive look at the gifts that often go unnoticed. The universe responds to gratitude with more blessings, as this practice opens doors to a constant flow of prosperity and harmony.

Developing intuition is another essential aspect of the Celtic journey. For the ancient Celts, intuition was an inner compass, a direct link to the wisdom of the spiritual world. Meditation and contemplation are valuable tools for sharpening this perception. Meditating outdoors, listening to the whisper of the wind or the sound of running water, helps to tune in to the subtle messages of nature. Observing patterns and signs - such as the appearance of a particular animal, the shape of the clouds, or the movement of leaves - can bring deep insights. Trusting one's instincts and listening to the inner voice are practices that strengthen this intuitive connection, allowing for clearer guidance in times of doubt or transition.

Magic permeates Celtic spirituality and is seen as the conscious manifestation of will aligned with the forces of nature. Incorporating magical practices into everyday life does not require large rituals; small gestures charged with intention already have immense transformative power. Creating a Celtic altar at home, with sacred symbols, candles, crystals, and offerings, establishes a space for spiritual connection. Using herbs in healing and protection rituals, such as burning sage to purify an environment or preparing chamomile tea to calm the mind, are simple ways to bring magic into the routine. Amulets and talismans with Celtic symbols, such as the Celtic knot or the triskele, can be used for protection and energy strengthening. Incantations and affirmations pronounced with intention have the power to shape reality, as words carry vibration and purpose. More than elaborate spells, true magic lies in awareness and respect for the natural flow of life.

Connecting with Celtic gods and goddesses is a path of learning and inspiration. Each deity has aspects and archetypes that reflect different forces of the universe and the human being. Honoring these energies can be done in a variety of ways: studying their stories and myths, dedicating symbolic offerings, or simply calling their names in times of need or gratitude. Brighid, for example, represents inspiration, healing, and the creative forge, being a powerful guide for artists and healers. Dagda, the father god, is a symbol of prosperity and protection. Morrigan, the goddess of sovereignty and transformation, teaches inner strength and courage to face change. The relationship with these deities is personal and can develop naturally as the spiritual connection deepens.

Living with honor and integrity is a fundamental principle on the Celtic path. Ancestral traditions value truth, justice, and respect for the bonds that unite all forms of life. This means acting ethically, keeping promises, being true to your words and choices. Respecting nature not just as a concept, but as a daily practice - reducing waste, treating animals with dignity, valuing every living element of the planet - is a manifestation of this honor. Seeking balance in all actions and relationships strengthens this harmony, making life a reflection of Celtic principles.

Finally, Celtic spirituality invites us to celebrate life in its fullness. Every day is a gift, every encounter carries meaning, and every experience can be lived with magic and enchantment. Dancing, singing, storytelling, expressing yourself creatively - all of this strengthens the connection to the sacred. Celtic music, with its ancestral melodies, awakens deep memories and resonates with the soul. Art, in any form, is a channel of expression of the divine. Sharing moments with friends and family, celebrating the cycles of nature, and living with joy are ways to honor this ancient tradition.

To integrate this spirituality into everyday life, some simple practices can be incorporated: creating an altar at home as a sacred space, wearing jewelry and amulets with Celtic symbols, reading about mythology and traditions, listening to Celtic music to connect with ancestral energy, celebrating seasonal festivals with friends and family, living in tune with nature, and expressing creativity spontaneously. Small gestures, charged with intention, transform life into a flow of magic and meaning.

By walking this path, a portal opens to ancestral wisdom and an existence full of beauty, connection, and harmony. Celtic spirituality is not just a set of beliefs, but a way of being in the world - with respect, gratitude, and a deep sense of belonging to the great cycle of life.

Following Celtic spirituality is, above all, allowing yourself to dance to the rhythm of life, embracing the magic present in every moment. There is no final destination, only a path of continuous learning, where the connection with nature, ancestors, and the sacred is renewed every day. By cultivating this perception, one discovers that spirituality is not distant nor restricted to grand rituals, but pulsates in the breath of the wind, in the flame of a lit candle, in the silence of a starry night. And so, by living it authentically, one honors not only the ancient Celts but also the deep essence that makes us part of this vast and mysterious fabric of existence.

Epilogue

We have reached the end of our journey through the magic of Celtic nature, a path that has led us through ancient forests, stone circles, sacred rituals, and encounters with gods and goddesses. We explored Celtic cosmology, with its three interconnected realms, and the importance of connecting with nature, ancestors, and the flow of life. We delved into the depths of Druidism, unraveling the secrets of Celtic priests and their ancestral wisdom. We met the Celtic pantheon, with its vibrant deities and its myths and legends full of teachings and inspiration.

We learned about the importance of natural cycles, celebrated in the eight festivals of the Wheel of the Year, and discovered how each festival invites us to honor the changing seasons, to give thanks for abundance, and to connect with the energy of the universe. We explored Celtic magic, with its spells, enchantments, herbs, crystals, and rituals, and understood how the Celts used magic for healing, protection, prosperity, and transformation.

Throughout this book, we sought to bring Celtic spirituality to everyday life, showing how we can integrate its teachings and practices into our daily lives. We saw how connecting with nature, meditation, working with the elements, moon magic, and celebrating festivals can help us live in harmony with the cycles of life, awaken our intuition, manifest our dreams, and connect with the sacred.

Celtic spirituality is a path of enchantment, of connection with the earth and the cosmos, and of awakening to the magic that resides within each of us. It is an invitation to live with joy, gratitude, and respect for life, honoring ancestral wisdom and cultivating a sacred relationship with the universe.

We hope that this journey through the magic of Celtic nature has awakened in you the curiosity, inspiration, and desire to deepen your knowledge and spiritual practice. May the ancestral wisdom of the Celts guide you in your search for harmony, balance, and connection with the sacred.

May the magic of Celtic nature be with you!

www.ingramcontent.com/pod-product-compliance
Lightning Source LLC
LaVergne TN
LVHW040050080526
838202LV00045B/3566